Pastor Well

A Guide to Faithfulness in Pastoral Ministry

Hershael W. York

Pastor Well: A Guide to Faithfulness in Pastoral Ministry
Copyright © 2024 by Southern Seminary Press
All rights reserved.

Published by Southern Seminary Press
2825 Lexington Road
Louisville, KY 40280

Southern Seminary Press is a division of The Southern Baptist Theological Seminary. All rights reserved. No part of this publication may be reproduced, stored in a retrieval system or transmitted in any form by any means, electronic, mechanical, photocopy, recording, or otherwise, without the prior permission of the publisher, except as provided by United States copyright law.

Cover design: John Zurowski
Internal design: Anna Vanden Brink
Initial transcription and editing from podcast *Pastor Well with Hershael York* performed by Travis Hearne

ISBN: 979-8-9906600-0-7

To Tanya York, who has selflessly, lovingly, patiently helped me Pastor Well

Contents

Introduction   6

Start Well   9
- Is God Calling Me? 11
- How Should I Talk to a Search Committee? 16
- How Can I Remain Content in Ministry? 22

Preach Well   29
- Is Expository Preaching the Only Way to Preach? 31
- How Much Time Should I Spend on Sermon Prep? 35
- Should I Include an Invitation at the End of Every Sermon? 39
- How Should I Preach Secondary and Tertiary Doctrines? 44
- How Should I Preach the Funeral of a Non-Believer? 48

Lead Well   53
- How Do I Build the Right Staff? 55
- How Can I Treat Church Staff Well? 59
- How Should I Respond When Others Disappoint Me? 64
- How Should I Respond When I Disappoint Others? 68
- Is a Pastor-Led Church or an Elder-Led Church Better? 71

Shepherd Well   79
- When Is a Child Ready to Be Baptized? 81
- How Should I Practice Church Discipline? 86
- How Should I Minister to Those with Same-Sex Attraction? 91
- What Are Permanent Disqualifications from the Ministry? 95
- Should I Marry Two Non-Believers? 99
- How Can I Lead a Missions-Minded Church? 103

Love Well   109
- How Can I Cultivate and Protect My Marriage? 111
- Should I Relocate My Family for a Ministry Calling? 116
- Should I Observe the Billy Graham Rule? 121
- What are the Expectations of a Pastor's Wife? 124
- How Can I Guard Against Pornography? 128

Finish Well   133
- How Can I Prevent Burnout in Ministry? 135
- Five Ministry Challenges I Didn't Anticipate 140

Introduction

My entire life has been spent with pastors. Not only was I born into a pastor's home, but I was deeply influenced by the hundreds of pastors I knew through the unending circuit of Bible conferences, revivals, church camps, and fellowship meetings my family annually attended. My whole world was attuned to the rhythms, raptures, pleasures, and pains of those who shepherd God's people. While still in college, I joined a church staff and have been in pastoral ministry ever since. I gained practical pastoral experience in the church and academic pastoral knowledge in the seminary. While fulfilling God's call as a pastor, for nearly three decades I have also taught thousands of students studying for the pastorate in hope that they might love the life that I have loved so passionately. Most of my friends are pastors. By God's grace, one of my sons is a pastor.

I simply do not know who or what I would be if Jesus had not allowed me to be one of his shepherds. Consequently, I think about pastoral ministry seven days a week, twelve months a year. I never tire of talking with pastors who are thinking through the challenges and opportunities they face. I love having conversations with those shepherds who are looking for answers because they desperately want to honor the Lord in everything they do, but they are facing challenges the Bible doesn't explicitly address and seminaries don't usually mention. In other words, I love talking with pastors about how to pastor well!

The Pastor Well podcast has been my attempt to apply a rich pastoral theology firmly rooted in the Word of God to the arduous, complicated, intricate challenges that pastors routinely face. I have always attempted to be entirely committed to the Word of God, but also willing to be painfully honest about how complicated ministry can be. I am, as I frequently confess, a pragmatist within my convictions. I will never compromise my convictions for the sake of convenience, but within my convictions, I want to know what works. What is the best course of action in any given situation? How can a pastor lead a church to practice church discipline without getting fired? What can a pastor honestly say without upsetting a grieving family when he preaches the funeral of an unbeliever? How does a pastor explain communion and who should partake of it? How much should a pastor tell his wife?

The articles in this book are taken from the recordings of the Pastor Well podcast. They have been only slightly edited and retain my natural conversational style. These were originally delivered with no manuscript but with years of experience and a heart full of love for God's servants. I hope this book still feels like I am sitting at your table talking about what it means to be an elder, an overseer, a pastor in one of the Lord's churches today.

May this small book yield big dividends in your life as you serve the Lord Jesus and care for the people he bought with his blood. May it give you strength for the journey and the confidence that, by God's grace and to his glory, you really can pastor well.

PART 1

Start Well

A Pastor and His Calling

1

Is God Calling Me?

How do I know if God is calling me? How do I know if God is calling me to a specific place or a specific type of ministry? I often receive questions like this. It's important to remember that God speaks in different ways.

I do not believe in direct revelation where God says to you, "Go to this church." You will never hear me tell my congregation, "I'm leading you to do this because God told me to." That kind of language is harmful because sometimes you might lead the church to do something with the best of intentions, yet it proves to be wrong, even disastrous. I once led a church to buy a piece of property; then the city denied us permission to build on it, and we had to sell it. Had I said, "God led me to that piece of property," and then it ended up being useless to us, my credibility would've been shot. I thought it was a good idea, and I said that; but I didn't claim God revealed it specifically and specially. So how *does* God reveal his will enough to take the next step into vocational ministry? I think there are five primary ways:

1. The Word of God
2. Desire
3. Gifting
4. Opportunity
5. Testimony of Others

The Word of God

The very first way God reveals his will is through his Word. God will never call you to do something contrary to what he has written in his

Word. He's never going to lead you to do something inconsistent with his revealed will. If a woman comes to me and says she is called to be a pastor, I must disagree with that immediately. God's Word teaches specific qualifications for a pastor, one of which she cannot meet because she is a woman. God certainly might be calling her to some other very important ministry, but he will not call her to fulfill a role whose qualifications she cannot meet. God will not call a man to be a pastor who is morally disqualified. That would be inconsistent with the Bible, and we must always look to the Word first of all. God's calling and God's Word will always be consistent.

Desire

The second way calling is revealed is through desire. God usually aligns our desires with the things that he wants us to do. Maybe there was something you didn't desire in the past, you didn't really want to do it, but then you feel your desire has shifted toward that ministry opportunity. God moves our will and plants within us a desire to do the thing he is calling us to do. We find the motivation to do it and even enjoy doing it. And that leads to the third way God reveals calling — gifting.

Gifting

If he calls you to do it, God will also enable you to do it by gifting you or at least providing an opportunity to acquire the skills you need to fulfill the task. By nature, I am an introvert. I very much enjoy being alone, but I realized I couldn't influence people very well hiding in my study reading a book. I must be with people. I had to trust the Holy Spirit to enable me to overcome my natural bent in order to touch people with the gospel.

If you feel God is calling you to do something that is difficult for you or even contrary to your personality, rest assured he'll give you the ability to acquire the skills that you need to do the thing that he calls you to do. It would make no sense for God to call you to do something and then never empower or enable you to do it.

Opportunity

The fourth way God reveals his will is through opportunity. It's inconceivable that God would call you to do something, enable you to do it, give you the desire to do it, but then give you no opportunity to do it. Sometimes the opportunity presents itself first, and *then* the Holy Spirit begins to shape our desire, giving us the desire to acquire the skills or gifting us in ways that may surprise us.

Maybe there was a time you dreaded the thought of getting up in front of people, but then when God called you to preach, you began to find joy in getting up and opening the Word of God and teaching people. When I say God provides opportunities, I don't necessarily mean that you get an engraved invitation.

When I went to seminary in Memphis, Tennessee, no one there knew me, and no one was going to invite me to preach simply because I showed up in the community. I made a commitment that I was going to preach somewhere every week whether I got invited or not. That meant I had to find places to preach for myself. I called the West Memphis Jail, the Shelby County Detention Center, a rescue mission, a nursing home, and a Catholic school for special needs children and asked if I could come and preach or tell Bible stories. When all else failed, I'd go down to the Mid-America Mall near downtown Memphis and stand on the street corner to preach. I made sure that at least once a week, usually twice, I preached somewhere.

After a few months, my new pastor and other people noticed I was serious about preaching, and I began to receive invitations to preach in churches. So, when I say opportunity is a mark of calling, understand that may mean that you have to look for opportunity to fulfill and hone your abilities. You can create opportunities. If God's calling you to do something and giving you that desire to do it, you can find the opportunity to do it.

Testimony of Others

The fifth way God reveals his will is through the testimony of others, particularly other believers, fellow church members, and the pastors who know you. If God calls you to do something, he's going to show others in your life and church family that you can do it. This is why baptist churches have the practice of ordination. The Bible says, "Lay hands suddenly on no man" (1 Timothy 5:22). In other words, we need to be tested first. The church must watch the lives of the people in the church to see what gifting they demonstrate. When God is dealing with a man and beginning to call him into ministry, it's not unusual for someone to approach him and ask, "Have you ever considered being a pastor?" or "Have you thought about going to seminary and training for ministry?" or some similar question. This may be a way of God revealing his will to you.

Five Ways in Concert

God's calling does not always come in any one way — it's usually a concert of feelings and events. His will for you is always consistent with his Word. You feel him giving you a desire to do something, perhaps a different desire than you've ever had before. He gifts you, enabling you to develop abilities and aptitudes that fit the sense of calling. He gives you opportunities, and other people bear witness to a fruitfulness that manifests itself when you serve. So think through these five markers. Are you sensing a consistency in them? When those things line up, it's a good indication that God may be calling you to vocational ministry.

But you need to ask yourself: Am I effective in this? Am I fulfilled in it? If we are doing the will of God, we will be fulfilled in doing the will of God. Certainly we may experience moments of frustration and doubt, but like Jeremiah, a "fire in my bones" makes us unable to walk away from the task to which God calls us. Are you being obedient to what God has shown you? God's not going to show you more if you're not being obedient to things that he has already shown you. I don't have to pray about whether God wants me to be a good husband. I don't have to pray about whether he wants me to be a man of prayer. I just need to do those things because he has already revealed those in the Bible. If I'm not doing the things that are clearly taught in his Word, he probably will not lead me to do something else. At the very least, my spiritual hearing is blocked, and I will be unable to hear and discern his will because I am not walking in the basic disciplines.

Conclusion

If you truly want to know God's will so you can obediently follow him, there is a single indispensable prayer you must pray. You must simply and sincerely beg God the Holy Spirit to help you bring glory to Jesus Christ. When that becomes your deepest desire and your greatest prayer, incredible things will happen in your life.

On the other hand, if you say to the Holy Spirit, "Oh Holy Spirit, I really want to be a great pastor," you might be surprised to discover that the Holy Spirit is not at all interested in that prayer. That is not the ministry of the Holy Spirit. You might ask the Holy Spirit to help you be a great author. The Holy Spirit yawns at that. That is not the ministry of the Holy Spirit. You might plead with the Holy Spirit to help you be an effective preacher, but the Holy Spirit does not really care about your pulpit skills. You can desire and ask for many good things, but none of them will move the Holy Spirit. The great task and ministry of the Holy Spirit is to glorify the Son, the Lord Jesus Christ, and to testify of him. So when you sincerely and desperately pray, "Holy Spirit, would you enable me to glorify Jesus?" that is when the Holy Spirit says, "Is that what you want? Because that is precisely what I want. That is my ministry. And if that's what you want, then I will enable you to do it."

When you begin to desire to glorify Jesus above all else, it is unthinkable that God, the Holy Spirit, will say no to that prayer. He will always help you glorify Jesus. He will never deny you the ability to glorify Christ. If you are living in that desire and dependence on him, the Holy Spirit will not let you make a wrong decision that leads you away from glorifying him. Make that your passion, and he promises to help you to fulfill his will. If you are a pastor, do it for the glory of Christ above all else, and that will help you pastor well.

2

How Should I Talk to a Search Committee?

I wish there were a more spiritual way for churches to find a pastor, but unfortunately few churches are raising up young men within their body who are obvious choices to assume the role of pastor. Optimally, a church might have within their own congregation or pastoral staff someone whom they know well and who has already distinguished himself as a called, gifted, and proven servant of Christ, and that choice can be made rather quickly.

I led the church I served for twenty years down that path with wonderful results. One of my associate pastors had served faithfully with me, had demonstrated his gifts and calling as well as his doctrinal fidelity, and several years before I actually stepped down as Senior Pastor, the church called him to succeed me upon my departure. Happily, it was a nearly unanimous vote of the members, and the changeover went beautifully — a "no drama, no trauma" pastoral transition. That is ideal, and frankly, it should be more common, but that is not what typically happens.

For one thing, it takes a church of enough size that they're able to have a pastoral staff and enough vision that they develop a pipeline of leaders over years. For another thing, the typical baptist church runs about seventy members, and they usually don't have anybody from within the congregation who meets the New Testament qualifications for serving as the pastor-teacher. They typically look for candidates outside of their congregation.

So how does the process normally work? Well, often they put an ad in some denominational paper or on some website that they're looking for a pastor, and they invite résumés, and the procedure commences there.

Search Committees Are Not Professionals

Now, there's nothing wrong or unspiritual about sharing résumés and letting churches know of your availability, but you need to know what will happen in a conversation with the search committee. What are the questions they'll ask, and what are the questions that you should ask? Before I answer that question, I'm going to make a claim that sounds odd, York's universal assessment of search committees: *They all do it badly.* Please understand, I don't say that critically. These people are amateurs. They don't get paid to search for a pastor. They all have families and jobs and a full life. Furthermore, they are under a lot of pressure, and most of them haven't done it before and therefore don't know how to do it. If they could do it well, that would only be because they've done it a lot, which on the contrary means they haven't done it well because they've not chosen anyone who stays very long. In a typical church, they only do this rarely because they must.

Sometimes they read someone's book that tells them exactly the process to follow. There might even be two or three books they read that give conflicting opinions and advice. They might feel unsure about the process. Should they be looking at five guys at once or just one at a time? In addition to their own questions and issues, they're dealing with the unique history of the church, and that can be challenging to a candidate. So my strong suggestion to all potential pastors is cut them some slack. You are the professional, not them. Allow them to make their mistakes and do things in ways that make no sense to you. Trust that nothing they do is outside of God's providence and ability to get the result he wants.

They often won't tell you things that you probably should have been told. They're just trying to finish their task. They're trying to conclude the search, and sometimes they forget to tell you certain things or do certain things, and sometimes they'll make guarantees that they simply cannot keep. This happens a lot, so I'm advising you to have grace toward a search committee. When you meet with them the first time, remember that they are completely in the driver's seat, not you, and you can't afford to get ahead of them. Don't assume you are their only candidate. Don't présumé that you are their perfect solution, no matter how badly you need the job or how much you long to be a pastor. Go into this with low expectations, humble and willing to answer their questions and to follow their process.

They probably will send you a questionnaire first. Try to find the balance between being as complete as you must be but as succinct as you can be. Be neither terse nor verbose. Short, truthful answers are your best strategy. When you meet in person they will ask you about your salvation experience and your call to ministry. They will examine your education. They will want to talk about your family, which the Bible gives them the right to do — don't ever forget that. They need to know that you lead your household well, and if you don't, that disqualifies you from being a pastor. They have the right to ask you those questions and to talk to you, and you need to honor them and their process. Don't correct them and say, "Well, it would be better if you did this." Just go into it with a smile on your face.

Learn Names

And here is the big secret. I am going to tell you one thing, and if you do it, it will make a massive difference and a positive impression — learn the names of everybody on that committee, and use their names when you address them, even if you have to write them down. Let them see that people matter to you.

It says a lot about a guy that he would even write a little chart of the committee members' names and where they're seated at the table. Even if you can't remember all their names and must look at your sheet now and then, that still says you cared enough to make an effort and to use their names. Your memory is less significant than the way you treat them. People like to know their names matter, especially for a pastor. Learn their names, and when you talk to them, answer their questions honestly.

Be Brief and Honest

Short truthful statements are your friend. If they ask you to explain your view of some doctrine, that does not mean you need to tell them everything you think. You do not need to give a lecture on the hypostatic union. It is usually enough to say, for instance, if you are a Southern Baptist, "I agree completely with the Baptist Faith and Message 2000, and I am happy to talk about any particular points within it if you want to, but I fit within the general framework of Southern Baptist conservative theology." Committees are afraid that they are going to call someone who believes something strange, weird, or harmful to the church. Therefore, locate yourself within the greater realm of your faith tradition, and then let them ask any specific questions. Answer truthfully and candidly, but don't say more than you need to say because you can get wrapped up in minor details that are not the kind of things a pastor is ever going to deal with.

Ask to See Important Documents

At some point, as the process moves along, and after they have asked you theological and practical questions, they'll let you know that you are a serious candidate to them. If they have not offered to give you their key documents at that point, it's proper for you to ask. But not too early — only after it's evident that they're seriously considering you. Otherwise you seem presumptuous. Remember that they are in charge of the speed of the process.

Once they let you know that you are being seriously considered to be their next pastor, you need to ask for a copy of their constitution and bylaws (if they have any!) as well as their annual church budget. If they're a Southern Baptist church and they have filled out an annual church profile, ask for a copy of that. You might be able to get that from their local association as well. The church profile provides all the key stats of that church: their attendance, their finances, their giving to the different missional causes, and the number of baptisms they have had. Those things are indicators of a church's health or lack thereof, and it's good for you to know. Are they in debt? If you're going to be the lead pastor, it's important to know if you're going to have to lead the church to pay off debt. Have they adopted any long-range plans such as buying property or planning to relocate? Are they expecting the next pastor to follow their adopted plans? You need to ask for those documents and have those conversations.

Ask Good Questions

At some point, they are going to ask if you have questions for them. The best way to start is to just go around the room, beginning with the quietest person on the committee, and ask each of them to answer. For example, ask for their opinion on what will be "the next pastor's greatest opportunity." Notice the way I suggested you ask that question. Don't put your question in the first person. Don't ask, "What would be *my* greatest opportunity?" That sounds presumptuous, like you already think you have the job. After the first person answers, thank them, and go on to the next person. Go around the entire table. Each of them will give you what they think the greatest opportunities are, and they won't give you one answer. You will probably hear different answers. That is why I recommend not starting with their chairperson but instead with a quiet person who gives his or her opinion. Then have each of them give theirs to hear the differences between them. After they have all answered, you will begin to get a picture of the opportunities ahead.

Then ask the second question: "What would be your next pastor's greatest obstacle that might stand in the way of making progress?" Again, start with someone other than the chairperson, then listen carefully to the answers. You will see certain fissures appear on the committee. They will have different opinions, but from the composite of all their answers, you will gain a significant glimpse into the inner issues of their church. As they tell you the obstacles and the opportunities, you will get an idea of how they perceive their church's history and future.

Then ask a third question: "What do you think should be your next pastor's first move when he arrives?" As they talk about these things, the picture of the church will come into sharper focus. A lot of times somebody will say something that seems strange or like a total outlier to you. Maybe something you didn't see coming. They'll say something like, "Well, he's got to take care of the sewer system." And you're suddenly interjecting, "Now, what? Can you explain?" That would not have been on your radar at all, but you discover there's a major problem with their building that's causing other issues. The outlying answer might be about something from within the congregation. Someone may say, "Well, they've got to decide on whether or not we're going to move or how we're going to reach an ethnic group that's come into the neighborhood." As you begin to hear different views, it's going to give you a picture of what's really going on in the church and how you should respond. Some of it may be discouraging, but that is precisely why God sends them a shepherd!

Not a Job Interview

Remember that the goal is not to get a job, but to discern God's will. The more you answer their questions and reveal who you are, and the more you ask questions of them and hear their answers, the more you're going to picture how you might work with them. What you're looking for is a fit. There are a lot of wonderful godly men who shouldn't be a pastor of some particular church just as there are a lot of godly women I might respect and admire, but I only "fit" one of them in marriage.

When a pastor and a church really "fit" together, it's a glorious thing. That's what you're looking for. Is it in the providence of God that you go to this church, that you be their shepherd, that you teach them the Word, and that you walk through life with them? As you begin to open this discussion with them, you are trying to learn if you are compatible with the church. These aren't exhaustive questions, but they're designed to help you think about how you can discuss this with a committee. The ultimate goal is to find the will of God, to follow where the Lord leads, to love his people, and to pastor well.

3

How Can I Remain Content in Ministry?

Effective ministry requires us to stay content in ministry and calling. Contentment is not merely the power of positive thinking. Contentment comes from knowing who we are in Christ and how that shapes the way we think about life, the way we approach ministry, and the way we treat other people. And of course, it starts in your most secret place — your heart.

The Misery Gap

Strive to develop an intimate relationship with the Lord Jesus Christ. In your most secret and private moments, the thing that you most desire and the outcome you desperately want must be to honor Jesus. There is a lot of turmoil in ministry because men are different in their private lives than in their public ministry. In private, they might indulge in pornography. In secret, they may be watching things they shouldn't watch and doing things they shouldn't do.

I call the gap between what we believe and how we live *the misery gap*. Whatever distance exists between the hard earth of our behavior and the high sky of our intentions will be filled with misery. The inconsistency breeds discontent, grief, anger, bitterness, and sorrow. We become surly and unhappy with ourselves. Ironically, we even blame God for letting us do things that we know are wrong, simultaneously having our own way and yet telling ourselves it's his fault because he should stop us.

You've got to make sure that in your most secret life, you're honoring the Lord. Who you are in secret is who you are. In your most private life, you need to love the Lord Jesus Christ more than self, more than sin, more than anything.

Take Control

When you're consistently trying to honor the Lord, you will be more joyful than when you are in the flesh. You can't control everything, but you must control what you can, and that's your time, your heart, your thoughts, and your behavior. You can't control the world around you, but you can control those things. You can control whether you're looking at pornography, how you speak to your wife and your children, whether or not you are in the Word of God. You cannot expect to be in control of your emotions and your demeanor until you've taken control of those things. When other things beyond your control happen and assault you, you can still experience a sense of peace and joy in the storm because what's in the center will hold firm. You must have a centered life and an intimate relationship with the Lord Jesus Christ.

Let your first moments of the day be spent in praise and prayer. Get in the Word and have a vibrant conversation of love with the Lord Jesus Christ. I get up very early in the morning, long before my wife, and I spend much time with the Lord reading the Word, praying, and worshiping. Those moments are absolutely precious and energize me for the day ahead. I have that time with the Lord, then when Tanya wakes up, I have that time with her. I intentionally design to make the first moments of my day happy and joyful with the Lord Jesus and happy and joyful with Tanya. It sets the tone and the mood for the entire day.

Find a Hobby

Another strategy that doesn't sound particularly spiritual, but is important nonetheless, is to have some kind of outside interest or a hobby. It needs to be something you enjoy and something you like to think about. John Stott was a hero of mine, and he was a famous bird watcher. He went all over the world just to hear and see particular birds and to hear them call. That was his thing.

I don't particularly relate to it, but I've got certain things that I pursue and enjoy very much. I enjoy travel and seeing the customs of other places. I find great delight in learning and attempting to speak other languages, however badly. I love reading all kinds of books. And I know this sounds weird, but I could tell you more about Greek vases than you would ever want to know. Don't even get me started on the Sarpedon Krater. I've got an obsession with Herod the Great, whom I find beyond fascinating. I've got every book on Herod that has been written in the past century. It's just a little niche that I like filling up. It focuses my mind on something that is not sinful or destructive, but outside of my normal world. You need something like that. Maybe it's hunting or fishing. It could be following baseball. There are a lot of wonderful things that you can do to interest yourself in the margins of life that will give you a break from the heaviness and relentlessness of ministry. It will help you maintain joy.

Be Grateful

I cannot imagine anybody's life being more blessed than mine. I honestly believe I'm the most blessed man you'll ever meet. I am God's spoiled child, but I am not an ungrateful child. I'm grateful every day, and I marvel at the ways God has guided my life. Even the things that I thought were disappointments turned out to be the grace of God. I learned a long time ago that my heavenly Father will deny me no good thing. Romans 8:28 is true and always in effect. Since all things in my life work together for good, because I am called by God and I love him, I know that he's working everything in my life for the ultimate purpose of conforming me to the image of his son, the Lord Jesus Christ. I can rest in God's providence and his care for me because I'm grateful that he has shown himself faithful. And when you're hurt so badly that it's hard to have a grateful spirit, look to the cross.

The cross is God's incontrovertible evidence that he's good to you, that he loves you, that he has provided for you. He gave himself for you. Even in your sorrow, your grief, and your overwhelming pain, the cross bears unrelenting witness to God's unfailing goodness. And you can be grateful that the sufferings of this present world are not worthy to be compared to the glory that shall be revealed in us. Rest in that.

Contentment

The late Jim Elliot wrote in his journal, "Wherever you are, be all there." That is great advice. It's easy for you to think, "Boy, if I had that advantage," or "If I could pastor a church like that," or "If I could have a large staff," or "If I could just have more money." It's easy for us to lust after things and circumstances we don't have. But God, who loves you eternally and boundlessly, put you right where you are because he is working everything together for your good. To covet or lack contentment is to deny God's love and provision. Peter wrote to his fellow elders to "shepherd the flock of God *that is among you*" (1 Peter 5:2). Don't shepherd someone else's flock. Don't shepherd the flock you wish you had. Shepherd the flock of God that is among you, the one God has given you, and be all there. Don't think about what it used to be somewhere else or what you wish it were. Be all there.

Don't compare yourself to others. I don't need to be anybody else. I teach at Southern Seminary with what I consider to be the greatest evangelical faculty in the history of theological education. I sometimes feel like Scooby-Doo at the Westminster Kennel Club. How did I get in here with these theological giants? But I don't have to be Albert Mohler or Tom Schreiner. I don't have to be any of these titans of the evangelical academic world. I just have to be Hershael York. And I'll never forget that I'm a boy from Julien, Kentucky (population 18!). And above that, I am a sinner. I'm amazed that God used me at all. But he is using me for one purpose only: to glorify himself. How and where I do that is God's business.

If you are comparing yourself to others and what they can do, how talented they are, what car they drive, or anything else, that comparison will make you discontented. But when you realize that God has given you everything you need for life and godliness through the knowledge of him who has called you to glory and virtue, you can let go of all discontentment. He has provided you all you need to serve him where you are.

A Prayer for Contentment

Lord, you've been so gracious to save me, to call me into ministry, and you didn't have to use me at all. You've kindly allowed the circumstances of my life that have driven me to Christ. And you've used these things to conform me more to his character and likeness. I am grateful to you, Lord. Please give me a spirit of joy and contentment so that the people around me see a delight in the things of the Lord in me, an enchantment in my relationship with Jesus Christ so that I'm not preaching and ministering out of books, education, or effort, but rather out of the overflow of my relationship and walk with Jesus Christ. And through that contentment help me to pastor well.

PART 2

Preach Well

The Pastor and His Pulpit

4

Is Expository Preaching the Only Way to Preach?

Nothing affects our shepherding like preaching. We are to feed and to lead. Frankly, you can't do that apart from preaching. Throughout my pastoral ministry I've been committed to teaching and practicing an expository preaching model. In other words, I like to preach through either large sections or entire books of Scripture. Though I may sometimes deviate, my normal method has always been to preach systematically through an entire book so that my church can understand what the author means, how it applies, and how it fits within the biblical story of redemption.

Expository Preaching as the Norm

My definition of expository preaching is very broad. I don't think it needs to be too ornate. Expository preaching includes any preaching that explains the meaning of the passage as the author intended and then makes appropriate application to the lives of the listeners. Expository preaching has only two non-negotiable elements: the correct meaning of the passage and appropriate application for the listeners. This kind of preaching gives your people a strategic grasp of the Scriptures and helps them see the way the Holy Spirit inspired and assembled it within the general historical redemptive arc of scripture.

But now here's the question I want to deal with specifically: is expository preaching the only legitimate way for a pastor to preach? That's a good question. I might surprise you when I say it's not the only way. Some occasions merit a topical sermon, almost like a conversation that a pastor must have with his church. It should never be separated from Scripture, but it's not necessarily going to be a systematic study through a book or one particular section. But the best week-in, week-out methodology for a pastor is expository preaching. That's what you want your people to expect and to grow accustomed to. I am convinced it's the way they will grow in the Lord most effectively.

As they deepen in their appreciation of the Word of God, they won't only become good listeners, but also good students. They're learning how to study the Bible as they consistently hear it taught systematically and purposefully. The way you handle the Word of God in the pulpit is the way they will handle the Word of God when they study it. So, you're always going to need to teach them these two things: the main point and the application. When you always show those two things in your sermon, they will learn always to locate those two things in their own Bible reading. They will learn to never go after something outside of the author's intention or never to major on the minors because they've heard it done well in the pulpit.

Topical Preaching When Necessary

While it's not wrong to preach the minor point of a passage, you should always practice "truth in labeling." Be clear and say, "The main point of this passage is _____, but I want us to examine a lesser, though still very important, point of the passage." For instance, let's say you're preaching on the prodigal son. If you only have one week to preach on the prodigal son, you really ought to make Luke's main point the main point of your sermon. But it's not improper, if you've got several weeks, to preach a sermon on the heart of the father. You would show them the main point of the text, that Jesus rebuked the Pharisees, but then say that you want everyone to notice something that Jesus tucks so neatly into this parable—a glimpse into the heart of the father. You are still teaching them to locate the main point first, even while seeing the depth and breadth of the truth in the text.

There are also times and events in the life of a church when a pastor must step aside from the typical preaching through a whole book of the

Bible to address maybe a church tragedy. I know of a pastor in a church where someone in their church accidentally ran over an infant at a church soccer game. When you have deep grief like that pervading your church family, it may not be a wise thing to just continue your series in Zephaniah while your whole church is hurting. They are all asking why things like that happen and why God would let it happen. To be a good shepherd, you may need to step aside from your preaching schedule and deal with your flock. Obviously, you should firmly root it in a text. It's topical, but it's not topical apart from a biblical text. You can look for a passage that you think addresses the issue, that reveals the truth about the subject, and then you need to teach it and make the application.

I can remember when 9/11 happened in 2001. I did some research to see what some well-known pastors did. Pastors like John Piper, John MacArthur, and others who were preaching the Sunday after 9/11 all departed from their planned series and preached to what was happening in the world. We all have recognized events in the life of our church, our nation, or our world where we need to do just that. That's good shepherding. You can't ignore these circumstances; you need to talk about them. You need to give your people a biblical lens to view the world and you are the person God has put there to do it. You're the shepherd who can show them how to address the big issues of life.

"Take Out the Trash" Sermons if Needed

There's another kind of sermon which I call a "take out the trash" sermon. Some homileticians suggest that every sermon must include a list of certain items to be faithful. And, in general, I might agree that's a good checklist for sermons. But sometimes an issue is so pressing, an instruction so desperately needed, that a pastor needs to just address it and tell his congregation what to do. When my sons were young and at home, I frequently told them I loved them. I wanted them to know every day and in every moment their dad loved them. But sometimes, when a chore was undone, I just said, "Take out the trash." I didn't tell them I loved them. I just said, "Hey, do this. Now." That conversation was within the framework of my love for them, but I didn't feel the need to express it explicitly. I had already done it — a lot. But now I just wanted them to take out the garbage. In every circumstance and in every conversation, pastors must recognize that we hang a framework about Christ and his work of redemption. But now and then you must have the kind of conversation with your church where you address something in your church, whether it's a tragedy, division, or something else. Maybe that sermon is not going to fit in your series or tick every box that you would normally tick. You certainly don't want to do that too often or it loses its effectiveness. If I step out of a series to address something like that at the church I serve, its rarity is what makes it powerful. You don't want it to be usual at all. But don't feel that if you don't check every box in every sermon you've somehow been less than faithful. See that sermon in the context of the previous ten sermons.

Lead and Feed

Expository preaching should be your bread and butter, your *modus operandi*. You need to preach the text, preach through books of the Bible, and preach large sections of it so that your people understand the framework of the text, what the author is doing with it, and how it applies now and then. You are the shepherd. That is part of leading and feeding the flock. And when you do it, you pastor well.

5

How Much Time Should I Spend on Sermon Prep?

I have been asked this question for all my teaching ministry: how much prep time is appropriate? If you're preaching a sermon, how long should it take you to prepare? Now, it's an unfair question for a lot of reasons because there are so many factors.

How Old Are You?

I am now in my seventh decade of life, and I've been a Christian since I was seven years old. I've been studying the Bible my entire life. My dad taught me the truth of Scripture when I was very, very small, and I studied Greek as an undergraduate and then as a graduate and then went to seminary and have been in the pastorate ever since. It doesn't take me nearly as long in my sixties as it did in my twenties. And if it did, that would indicate a memory malfunction! My preparation time is shorter because throughout my entire life I've been building up a storehouse, and I've been putting things in that storehouse, and there aren't many passages of Scripture I haven't preached before. There are a few, but not many. So, one factor of sermon preparation time is how long you've been studying and preaching.

Are You Bi-Vocational?

It's also not fair for a bi-vocational pastor to think that he's got to spend as much time preparing a sermon as someone who has the luxury — and by the grace of God, it is a luxury — to be full-time in ministry. I would never want anyone to feel guilty because they don't have twenty hours to prepare for a Sunday morning sermon. The reality is, you must do what you can with the time that you have available.

Are You a Perfectionist?

Perfectionism is dangerous. In my whole life, I've never preached a sermon as well as I wanted to. And most of the time, perhaps 90% of the time, I step out of the pulpit with an overwhelming sense of failure. It's rare indeed that I think, "That went well." I usually think, "Oh, you forgot this," or "You didn't say this. Why did you blow it?" I am very, very critical of my own preaching. That kind of perfectionism can be intimidating and overwhelming in the pulpit or the study.

For instance, there's a phrase in Romans 7:9 where Paul uses the first person: "I was once alive apart from the law; but the commandment came, sin revived, and I died." And everybody asks who he's talking about. I believe Paul is writing and uses the first person because he's talking about Paul. In studying that, however, you can read several commentaries that say Paul was talking about Adam. You can read several others that say he's talking about Israel. And frankly, you could go down a rabbit hole on just identifying the "I" in Romans 7. Who is speaking? Is it Paul? Adam? Or Israel? You could go down that hole reading dozens of sources, and before you know it, you've spent all your time on that single issue.

But is it going to help you preach a better sermon and deliver the sermon better? You could get so caught up in details and different theories about esoteric things that you miss the big picture. So, if you have perfectionistic tendencies, you need to lay those aside and realize that the task is to teach the meaning of this Scripture.

So How Long?

If you pin me down and ask how much time I spend on a Sunday morning sermon, my first answer is an accurate answer — my whole life. I've spent my whole life preparing for that sermon. But at this age, I probably spend eight to ten hours in sermon preparation for a Sunday morning sermon.

My methodology, especially in the New Testament, is to translate it by working through the Greek text. I'm going to notice the strange things and look at textual variants. Then, I do a basic outline of how I think it breaks down and the major movements. I'll ask, "What are the main points he's making?" or "What's the application of this?" Then, I put it in a sermon form. Only at the end do I look at commentaries, and it's always delightful to learn that these brilliant scholars agree with me! It's also a little disconcerting when I see that I missed something there, or they're saying something differently than I am, which takes some time to rethink or correct. But through all of that, the main thing I must keep in focus is the truth of the text and the people I'm preaching to.

Picture as You Prepare

I would encourage you to picture the people in your congregation as you prepare. Think of that car mechanic, the public-school teacher, the farmer, the bank teller, and the single mom. Picture people because you're not preaching for a bunch of scholars. You're preaching for real people with real needs. If you breathe prayers for them as you prepare to serve them the Word, it helps you stay focused. And the focus should always be on application, not merely meaning. How does this change their life? You want to ensure you're not digging so deep that you have no breadth, and you don't want to be so broad that you have no depth. Look for that sweet spot so they can understand it, see it for themselves, and know how to apply it.

Always locate the main point and application. That's what you're going for. Don't feel guilty if you're a bi-vocational pastor and don't have ten hours a week for a Sunday morning sermon. Give it what you can. Use the available time that you have. Listen to the scripture while you drive and while you work. Listen to other people preach it, but don't copy their sermons. Listen to their take on it and how they go at it. You can find ways to use all the available moments to saturate your mind with the text and then do your best work. In the end, it's not about how much time you spend. It's about whether you're saturated with that Word.

A Stewardship

Sermon prep is ultimately about your stewardship of the time God has given you. You may not have 10 hours to spend on a Sunday morning sermon, but you want to use what you have. If someone tells me they spend forty hours a week on a sermon, I wonder what they are failing to do. A lot of shepherding must happen outside of your sermon prep. You want to make sure you maintain that balance, but use what you have. Use it well. By the way, a Sunday night or a Wednesday night Bible study will get quite a bit less than I put into Sunday morning. I will preach to many more people, specifically more lost people, on Sunday morning than any other time, so it will get most of my time.

Saturate yourself with that text and pray for the people of God to whom you will open this Word. God will bless it. The goal is never that people leave going, "Oh, I'm so glad I have a pastor who's an expert. I'm so glad I have a pastor who can tell me what this means." The goal is for them to leave, saying, "Oh, I see that in the text. I understand because he didn't just teach me the meaning of the text. He taught me how to read the Bible." That's what we're after. Bring them with you in your discovery of the meaning of the text because we don't want them to just lean on us. We want them to be self-feeders. And if you teach them that, then you will pastor well.

6

Should I Include an Invitation at the End of Every Sermon?

Should a pastor give an invitation at the end of a sermon, and should he do it every Sunday? I realize that this is somewhat controversial, and I want to talk through it. Let me begin by saying that I believe in giving a gospel invitation just about every time I preach. Any time I have a strong suspicion that lost people are present, I will give some kind of a gospel invitation.

The Objections

I know the objections. Let's talk about why people don't like it. First, we've all heard of or seen what I would call manipulative invitations. Well, if it's manipulation, it's not an invitation. It's manipulation. I am against any kind of trickery or any kind of pressure or psychology to get people to come forward. That kind of manipulation is what I call the "if you love your mother" invitation. That's phony. That's not a gospel invitation. That has nothing to do with eternity. That's not what I advocate. It's not honest, and it's harmful to the gospel.

People know when they're being manipulated, and they rightfully resent it. Pastors will say, "If you think God might be speaking to you, would you raise your hand? Now if you raised your hand would you take one step out in the aisle? Now, would you come forward?" That's just not what we see in the New Testament, and I don't think that is an honest invitation.

A Response

We should clearly and honestly invite people to put their faith and trust in Jesus Christ as Lord and Savior. Now, that may look different in various contexts. There's no one way to do that, but I have a great biblical example. When Peter preached on Pentecost, at the end of his sermon, his listeners asked a question: "What shall we do?" Peter had an answer for them. He didn't say, "Well, let's sing a hymn, and if you still feel like you need to do something on Tuesday afternoon, contact me or email me, and we'll talk." He told them what they needed to do right then and there. And right then and there, they responded. They believed, they repented, and they were baptized.

It's always proper to tell people how to respond to the sermon. What response does this text demand and what will that look like in their lives? I always like to give what I call a long-term response. I'll explain how the text should affect their lives and behavior from now on. That will be drawn from the text, and I will show them a specific way that will take shape. But then I will ask them to make an immediate commitment, a decision right now, to seal it in their hearts. That doesn't always mean some physical response, though it may be. It might be coming forward to waiting pastors or counselors, lifting a hand so someone will come to them, going to a particular place in the building immediately or as soon as the service is over — there are many ways to give people an appropriate opportunity to respond that has no element of pressure or manipulation.

Public Decisions

If we convince ourselves we have made a decision in our heart and mind but don't tell anybody, by mid-afternoon that resolve may be gone. The Bible talks about confessing with our mouths. If God is stirring someone to respond to the message, I like to give them several ways that they can respond. I walk through several means to respond immediately at the end of that service. One is to walk forward. I'm aware that as our culture has changed, this is less likely than it used to be. People who grew up in a church culture saw people responding during an invitation, and they were freer to do so.

Coming forward is not the only way we tell people they can respond. I always say at the end of a sermon that our pastors are standing up in the front, and anyone can come and talk to them about what God is doing in their heart and their lives while we sing a concluding song. If it's a woman, we have godly women that will talk with them, or if it's a family, a pastor will do it. We take them into an adjacent room to find out what is troubling them. Is God convicting them of sin? Are they wanting to unite with our church in membership and what do they think God is leading them to do? We find out a little bit about their background and their spiritual background, whether they have placed their faith in Christ, and we tell them exactly how to know that they have. We find out about their baptism, and all of this is based on their response if they came forward.

If anyone prefers, I also issue an invitation to fill out a card near the seat. They can give it to any of the pastors or greeters after the service, or they can put it in the offering box as they leave to give us contact information, and then we follow up with them during the week. They are also free to email us or call us on their own during the week. So at the conclusion of the service, I've given them at least four ways they can respond: they can come forward, give us a card and put it in the box, come up to one of us personally afterward, or call or email. And yes, I do believe that God the Holy Spirit is at work, so I don't feel like I have to manipulate them in the least. I am not interested in anything but a genuine work of the Holy Spirit.

Don't Leave Them Frustrated

God uses his Word to shape and mold us, to conform us to the image of our Savior. And sometimes, that conforming feels powerful and obvious. If the Holy Spirit is working right then, people need to respond and voice that to someone. If I tell them they need to yield and surrender to what the Holy Spirit is doing, yet I give them no opportunity to speak it, I've only frustrated them. Many times I've seen people respond at the end of a service, and the thing on their heart has little relationship to the sermon. That used to bother me, but it dawned on me after many years that God the Holy Spirit does a whole lot of work outside of my sermon. They could be listening to someone on the internet. God could be working in their life through other people they work with or in their family. Many things could have happened to them during that week that brought them to church with a burden and a need to respond. Maybe I'm preaching a sermon on fathers not provoking their children to wrath, but God has been working in their heart about salvation. Why would I not give them an opportunity to speak to someone and have godly counsel in how to repent and believe?

No Pressure

There's no pressure. I'm not saying that if someone won't respond publicly, they aren't saved, nor am I assuming that if they walk an aisle and shed tears, they are regenerate. This is why we want to talk to them. But it is one way of many ways we tell people how they can respond.

Conclusion

I'll also point out that the primary purpose of the song we sing at the end of the sermon is not to invite people to trust Christ. The primary purpose of the music at the end of the sermon is to reflect on what was preached and to proclaim the glory of Christ in that text. It always has something to do with the text. Our congregation always sings more robustly after the sermon than before! It's usually some statement of the truth of the text in song, so we don't sing the traditional invitation hymns. It's usually not "Just As I Am." It's something like, "Come Behold the Wondrous Mystery." Or it's some song about praising Jesus for what he's done in the gospel. And 98% of it is our people just absolutely adoring Christ. And that's the best invitation you can give. When lost people see saved people rejoicing in the truth of the gospel, it's compelling. They feel the absence of something that others have.

Just be clear about what you are asking them to do. Don't merely ask them to "come forward", and never equate walking an aisle with coming to Jesus. Say, "Our invitation is very simple. Just respond to what the Holy Spirit is leading you to do, and our pastors will help you." We want to help them find out precisely what God is leading them to do, whether it's to put their faith and trust in Jesus Christ or deal with a sin issue or ask forgiveness from someone. Maybe they need to be biblically baptized.

We'll walk through that with them. But this is one opportunity for them to do it. When you combine an invitation to people with the worshipful musical response of your worshipers, it's a wonderful way to conclude the service. You see God at work in the lives and hearts of the saved and those he is saving or bringing back to himself. It's an incredible moment. And when you see that, I think it excites you to pastor well.

7

How Should I Preach Secondary and Tertiary Doctrines?

I want to talk about whether you should preach firmly about secondary and tertiary issues. Now, what do I mean by that? Dr. Albert Mohler has very helpfully talked about what he calls theological triage.[1] Theological triage divides doctrines into three tiers.

Theological Triage

First-tier doctrines are the things that define Christianity, things like the doctrine of the Trinity. If you don't believe in the Trinity, you're a heretic. It is a true first-tier issue. There's no compromise on first-tier issues.

Second-tier issues would be very important and denominationally define us. It would include things like the mode of baptism. I don't believe that everybody who believes in baptizing babies is an unbeliever. It's not a first-level issue, but it's very important. It defines who we are as baptists, and it's extremely important in our church. That's not optional for baptists. Immersion is the mode, and believer's baptism defines us. We're not saying everybody else who does something else is lost, but it does define us denominationally. It's a doctrine we adhere to because we believe it's definitionally important.

A third-tier issue would be issues that we could differ about within the same church. I personally think eschatology is third-tier. My dad was a

---

1. R. Albert Mohler, Jr., "A Call for Theological Triage and Christian Maturity," albertmohler.com, July 12, 2005, https://albertmohler.com/2005/07/12/a-call-for-theological-triage-and-christian-maturity

dispensationalist, and I am a historical premillennialist. We joked about it, but it didn't divide us in any way. My dad and I were members of the same church. I was his pastor for seven years, and we loved one another. We never had a cross word about eschatology, which is probably how it should be with most people. Some people make it a much bigger issue, but I think it's a third-level issue.

Preaching Triage

So, here's the question: how firmly should I preach these things that are secondary or third-level issues? Well, for secondary issues, I think within your church, you need to be really clear that these don't define Christianity, but they do define your church. These things are not optional for membership in our church.

Someone can be a Christian and believe in baptism by sprinkling, but they can't be a member of Buck Run Baptist Church and believe it because that defines us. It's very important, especially in these days of nebulous Christianity, that we define ourselves and have a clear statement of our faith. We need to let people know the basics of our faith when they come into our church because, frankly, if we're not clear on these things, you could eventually have a large group of people in your church who really don't believe the defining doctrines of your church. That could be problematic if a baptist church, for instance, did not talk about believer's baptism and treated it like a non-essential issue, acting like it's a third-level issue instead of a second-level issue. Eventually, you won't have a baptist church. You'll just have some amalgamation or some sort of ill-defined group of Christians, but it will not be a church that coheres because of doctrine, and if it doesn't cohere because of doctrine, it won't cohere long.

But I will also preach third-level issues with conviction when I think the text I am preaching warrants it. I am clear and resolute in my personal conviction, but I also explain that people in the church who don't see this as I do are welcome. I try to do that with eschatology and certain points of my soteriology. I, for instance, believe in what's sometimes called a limited atonement or particular redemption, but not everybody at Buck Run believes that. We don't divide over the extent of the atonement. We all believe that Jesus died for those who would repent and believe in him, and that's in our doctrinal statement, but we don't go beyond that. Now, when I preach, I will be honest with a text. I will preach the text and the doctrinal implications in the way that represent what I believe the text says, but I am also going to make sure that people who see it differently than me and who are faithful are welcomed in our church.

The way I explain it is this: there's a big difference between teaching something differently than me and teaching against me. I once had an executive pastor who was not as reformed as I was in his soteriology. We never once had a problem, and it would not have bothered me if he were teaching a class and mentioned that he interpreted a passage differently than I do. That's not a problem. If he says that I am wrong and exhibits an angry or contentious spirit, that's a different thing. If we teach these doctrines with an irenic spirit and an open heart and establish that we believe what the Scripture says but acknowledge there are faithful brothers and sisters within our church that see things differently, we are still unified by truth.

Preach with Conviction, Not Confusion

As a practical matter of preaching, I don't think it's usually good if you're preaching the book of Revelation to go through every passage in Revelation explaining all four views people hold on the passage. First, you'll wear people out. Secondly, you'll confuse them. They can't follow along. Preach it your way. At one time, I talked to Adrian Rogers about this, and he told me that he had toyed with some other eschatological views but that when he preached in his pulpit, he was 100% dispensationalist. I can affirm that he was indeed, but he was much more open to discussing some things in private conversation. When he preached it, however, he wasn't willing to confuse people. He thought this was right, and he taught it that way, and I think that's the best way to do so.

You need to be clear about what you believe and why you believe it when you teach those third-level issues. I also think you need to ensure you don't teach your preferences as though they were doctrines. I grew up in a group of churches in which I often saw personal preferences become doctrinal conviction. When I was a young boy, my father pastored a church that had been against air conditioning because they saw it as a worldly enticement to get people to attend church. My dad wisely suggested we should get rid of the furnace, too, if that were the case. If it was wrong to keep people cool in the summer, surely it was wrong to keep them warm in the winter! That silliness can often be taught as though it's what the Bible commands. That same church didn't allow missionaries to show slides because that was "worldly entertainment."

You might have certain preferences like that, but don't teach them as though they're the Bible because those are applications and preferences that are nowhere in scripture. Be clear and honest about where the true biblical lines are. Be clear about your opinion and interpretation, and don't divide over the things that are not defining issues. Be very, very clear, and when you do that, you help people know what you believe. You help them learn to understand the Bible in the way it should be understood, and that will help you pastor well.

8

How Should I Preach the Funeral of a Non-Believer?

Preaching the funeral of someone who was a faithful member of the church, whose life was a testimony of their faith in Christ, is a joyous, glorious occasion. It sounds odd that I enjoy funerals more than weddings, but I do, because people who attend are dialed in and extremely attentive. At a funeral, you get to preach to a new audience of people who wouldn't normally come to your church — or any church. At a wedding, however, they're all focusing on other things. Usually, even if you do preach the gospel at a wedding, trust me on this: nobody's really listening. But at a funeral, they are listening intently.

When you're preaching the funeral of a believer, it's sort of easy. You just talk about their faith, and you give examples from their life. But what about when you're not so sure? What about when you're preaching the funeral of a person whose name was on your church roll or someone else's church roll, but their manner of life left deep suspicions that they weren't a follower of Christ? Allow me to give you some advice.

First of all, don't assume you can truly know anybody's spiritual condition. I'm convinced that in heaven there'll be two big surprises: who's there, and who's not. There will be people that you thought were saved, but they're going to be the ones about whom Jesus said, "Depart from me, workers of iniquity, I never knew you," even though on this earth they said, "Lord, Lord." But there will be the five o'clock workers, the thief on the cross, the person who made a deathbed confession you didn't know about or to whom God brought a gospel memory, and they trusted Christ in a way and at a time that you didn't know.

Honor the Deceased, Help the Living

You can't really comment with any certainty about someone's eternal condition, so you certainly should not pronounce them damned in hell. That's not helpful or comforting to the family, even if it's true. First, because you can't actually know it. And secondly, because it's not helpful to the living.

I suggest that in every funeral you follow a certain pattern. At almost every funeral you preach, somebody loved that person, and you can celebrate the life and the person that the people around him loved to that extent regardless of their spiritual condition. Life is a gift of God, and they bore his image, so they should be celebrated. Usually, it goes in four steps.

First, in the simplest and most human sense, you can say he was a good man. Secondly, he worked hard. Whatever job he did, people liked to brag on whatever work he did. Thirdly, he loved his family. Most funerals you preach, people will be crying, and there's a testimony that there was affection and love between this deceased person, however flawed he may have been, and his family or someone. And fourth, there's almost always some kind of a comment about his hobby, his sports fanaticism, or something earthly that he loved — his favorite team or fishing or something like that. It's never improper for a eulogy to follow those general contours. But how do you then pivot to the gospel?

Pivot to the Gospel

Let's say he made a profession and was baptized in a church years ago, but you've got your suspicions that he wasn't really a follower of Christ because he hadn't been in church for decades. Here's the best thing to say: "*It was Jim Bob's testimony* that he had trusted Christ, and he showed that through his public profession and baptism." Now, that's as much as you can say, and that's really all you need to say. It was his testimony that he had trusted Christ. You are not saying it was genuine nor are you saying he died and went to hell.

Then you can pivot to the gospel by saying something like, "As we're gathered here to comfort one another in our grief and to pay our last respects, it's a reminder that there's going to be a service like this for every one of us, and we need to be ready. Scripture tells us how to be prepared for death." And then you just move right into the gospel, whatever your text is. You must be absolutely clear about the gospel when you preach at a funeral. Nothing unnerves me quite like attending a funeral where whoever's conducting the funeral never gets around to the gospel.

If you're preaching a funeral — *preach* the funeral. Preach the gospel. Every one of us must be ready. Share your gospel text and give the plan of salvation. Tell people what they must do, what they need to know about the death, burial, and resurrection of Jesus, that they must repent and place their faith in Christ and call on him. And then invite them to do so right there. As you close the service, invite them silently, right where they're sitting, to call on the name of the Lord in repentance and faith. Now, if the person had no testimony of faith whatsoever, you can do much the same thing. Just leave out the part about his testimony, and celebrate his life — usually, the family will share the details about the person with you — and then tell them that we all need to be ready to face death.

I love to preach the text of the Thief on the Cross. It's probably my favorite sermon text. I just talk about what Jesus revealed about the other side of death when he said, "Today you'll be with me in paradise." It's a great gospel text. It shows that there's personality beyond death. *You* will be with *me* in paradise beyond death. There's a place: paradise. There's a person: Jesus is there. The four most comforting words in the Bible are "With me in paradise." The thief on the cross, in his humility, recognized who Jesus was, that he was the king, and that he was going to sit on a throne. Jesus saw his faith and counted it as righteousness. Nothing shows the sovereignty of God quite like snatching someone from the very mouth of hell and taking him to heaven with him. Jesus did that. You just share the gospel like that and call on them to repent and to believe. Invite them to trust Christ.

They *Are* Listening

You might think nobody's really listening at a funeral, but they are. They're facing death. They're facing the reality of death. Years ago, I preached the funeral of a young woman who worked at a hospital in Lexington, Kentucky. At that point, it was the largest funeral attendance I'd ever preached to. For many years after that funeral, doctors and nurses in that hospital would stop me and say they needed to tell me that they trusted Christ at Phyllis Underwood's funeral. I'll never forget it.

God uses the gospel. The gospel has power. So, make sure that you are clear and distinct in your presentation of the gospel and tell people how to place their faith in Christ, tell them what they need to do in obedience after they trust Christ, and then let the Holy Spirit do his work. There's nothing more important than preaching the gospel. And when you preach a funeral, you have access to many people who would not darken the door of your church otherwise, but they'll be there at that funeral, and they will sit in silence and listen to you preach. That's your golden opportunity to share the gospel and see the power of the Holy Spirit and the Word at work. When you do this, you will pastor well.

PART 3

Lead Well

The Pastor and His Staff

9

How Do I Build the Right Staff?

How do you choose the right staff? How do you find a person that fits? How do you get your church to add a staff position? All these things come into play as your church grows. Many pastors begin in a small church and often are the only staff member, but if the Lord blesses and your church grows, you must make decisions about the staff.

Building a Staff

What position do you add first? Many pastors would immediately default to a worship leader as the first position to add. There's a calculation you need to make about what your church needs the most. It might be that a good office assistant would be a great help to you. Ask yourself: What would make you more productive? What would make your church more effective? What would add more people to your church? What would help you reach more unsaved people? It might be a worship pastor. It might be someone to lead your students. It might be an office assistant. You must ask yourself what you need. Another way to put this, though, is that you should choose staff to cover for your weaknesses. It might surprise you to know that when I began in ministry at 19, I was a minister of music and youth. I led the choirs and the worship and really enjoyed doing that.

Years later, I went to seminary. When I accepted the role of pastor at a little church in eastern Arkansas, I frequently found myself leading music simply by using my voice, sometimes over the song leader, just to keep things moving. Sometimes, I would lead the choir or a youth choir, because that was something that I had the ability to do. There were other things that I couldn't do, and I needed an office assistant to do those things. In my case, it made more sense to add that kind of staff position. In your case, it might be something else. This is why I encourage you to evaluate who you are and staff according to your weaknesses. You want to get someone who can do things you can't do well, and you need to respect your church's polity in how you do this.

If your church has never had another staff position, you must lead them to see the need and become willing to step out in faith and do it. You can't do that unilaterally. I don't care how much leadership credibility you think you have; you really must get them on board and persuade them. If you don't, it won't go well. And it would be unfair to the person you bring in if you don't. If you bring in someone and the church resents it, then that has a toll on that minister and his family, and they really did nothing to deserve that.

You need to do the groundwork. You need to find out the way your church thinks about a staff. Do they see the need? One of the key concepts of pastoral leadership is influencing the influencers. John Maxwell tells the story of how he pastored his first church in Indiana, and a gentleman named Claude was the longtime key lay leader in that church. Maxwell realized that he had to convince Claude if he wanted anything done. He would go out on Claude's farm and walk around with him and talk to him and ask Claude things like, "Have you seen how bad the front door is looking?" And Claude would say, "Yeah, preacher, I have thought that. Maybe I'll bring that up at the business meeting." And Maxwell learned that if he just influenced the influencer and he let Claude bring it up, the board would always go along with it. You can probably identify the key leaders in your church and begin to talk to them about the need. One other important detail: they must see that you are fulfilling your duties and working hard, or they won't be keen on adding somebody else.

This only works when they see the pastor's diligence. When you are really delivering the goods in the pulpit, they see that you're committing time; you're making it worth their while to come. You're visiting people that they've got to be able to see and identify. You must show a clear commitment to work. Then, when you're asking for help, they will understand it because they see you're busy. But if they can't see your investment and can't track the effort you're making, they won't want to add someone else. You've got to work diligently. You've got to work yourself into the need for another position. You've got to make the case for that position and get the church on board. Don't forget to respect their polity. The longer you are in a church, the more you understand their polity and can work within it. They also will trust you more, and you'll get a little bit more freedom in choosing staff.

Choosing the Right Staff

Let's say you put together a personnel committee, and this committee will help you choose a staff member, and so you initiate a search. Maybe you post on certain websites that you're looking for someone to fill this position, and you get résumés. They can help you sort through those. They can help listen to sermons or lessons or go and visit those people, whatever the case may be. Work with a leadership team to identify candidates. But first and foremost, you want to find someone that is doctrinally compatible. You don't want to get someone who will come in and have a totally different doctrinal outlook than you and your church.

Secondly, they need to philosophically be where you are. Some people can tick every box of theology I hold to, but they're not a philosophical fit. For instance, there may be some particular doctrine that is paramount to them, and everything else takes a backseat to their pet issue, and they want to talk about that thing all the time. That would wear me out! I can't take somebody who just flies the flag of their single focus, whatever it is. The pastorate demands a broader vision than that.

Also, I want to make sure that they are a personality fit. I don't want somebody a lot like me, or else one of us is unnecessary. I want people who are different than I am and have different gifts and skills. And so, if there's someone that's a little bit more of a methodical thinker than I am, a little bit less impulsive than I may be, that's a good balance to me. If they fit in doctrine, philosophy, and personality, then this is someone worth talking to.

Then, make sure to ask the right questions. Ask how they fit and how they will do the job and see themselves in that role. Also, let your people listen to them. Do everything you can to discover all these things upfront as much as possible so that before the decision is made, you've taken as many variables out as you possibly can for their sake and for yours. But then, once the decision is made, get behind them. If you really spend the right kind of time upfront trying to vet candidates to see if they fit you and your church culture, that they are doctrinally and philosophically sound, you'll save yourself a lot of headaches.

I want to emphasize that in the climate that we're in these days, you can't take things for granted. You need to do a background check. You need to do a credit check. You need to talk to their references. You need to ask people what they were doing in the church when nobody was paying them to do it. All those things matter. And then when you have a good assurance that you know this person and how they're going to fit, you bring them on the staff, and you work together for the church's growth and the glory of the Lord.

The Lord Provides

I look back to my very first hire. I prayed that the Lord would lead me to someone who would have his heart knit with mine in ministry. God led me to a man who came along beside me, ultimately served with me in two churches, and is a dear friend of this day. I thank God that he supplied me with what I needed at the time. So, if you pray, seek the Lord, and take these steps, it will help you get the right person; and then that person beside you will help you pastor well.

10

How Can I Treat Church Staff Well?

Few things are as significant in pastoral ministry as the way we get along with and treat pastoral staff and other staff members. If you are in a church that grows, and you add staff, you might eventually have other pastoral staff, office staff, worship leaders, youth directors, janitors, building managers, bookkeepers, IT staff, and perhaps any other job you can envision. If you're going to serve the Lord well, you need to know how to treat them, get along with them, and respect them. There are a few things that I've learned through the years that have helped me manage, befriend, encourage, and serve the Lord faithfully and effectively with my staff.

Be Convictional

Be clear and convictional. You don't want anybody who works for you to wonder what you believe about key issues of the day, specifically about your ecclesiology and the way things should be in the church. Great leadership arises out of conviction. You really can't lead if you're not convictional. Leadership is based on core beliefs and core convictions. In an era, for instance, where we're facing so many issues about sexuality and gender, you can't hope that your staff will guess what you think about these things or wonder how you would teach these things. You've got to be conspicuously, consciously, clearly convictional.

Be Predictable

Furthermore, you need to be predictable. Sometimes, people think that predictability is a bad thing. I argue exactly the opposite. I think predictability is one of the greatest marks of good leadership because when you are clear in your convictions and very predictable in your reactions and in your demeanor, people know how to make decisions even when you're not present. If people who work with me and for me are sitting in a room wondering what I would think on an issue, that means I've failed because I've not been clear in my convictions and commitments.

For instance, I want my associate pastors to know the kinds of things that do not bother me at all, so they don't need to worry about me being uptight. I also want them to know that I would not tolerate any abuse, dishonesty, disrespect, or immorality. I want them to know that I want to be consistent, not just in my convictions but in my reactions and responses. I think pastors need to take volatility out of their ministry. You don't need to pop off. You don't need to explode. You don't want to be that kind of man. You want to be calm and cool. My mantra is to never let them smell fear or anger on you. Those emotions seldom have any place in a pastor's life. But when you're clear, convictional, and predictable, they are empowered to make decisions even when you're not there because they know what matters.

To put a finer point on it, be especially predictable in two areas. The first one is convictions. I lead by conviction and from conviction, and I do not compromise on issues of true biblical conviction. I distinguish that from preferences. There are certain preferences I have that I don't claim are biblical, and I try to distinguish between the two. That leads to the second area we think about, and that is what I would call pragmatism. What works? I'm never going to compromise my convictions for pragmatism, but within my convictions, I'm always asking what the best thing to do is. What accomplishes what we want it to accomplish best? How can we do this to get the task done in a way consistent with our beliefs?

I'm going to confess here. I was the senior pastor of Buck Run for twenty years, but I don't think I went to a finance committee meeting more than twice in my last seven years. It wasn't because I didn't care about our finances, and it's certainly not because I ignored them. That would be at my own peril. It's that my finance team and my executive pastor knew the convictions by which I had led, and therefore they knew the pragmatic kind of application that I wanted to make in our church. I didn't have to be there. They were never going to cut our missions giving. They knew that violated my convictions and the convictions established by our church, so to my knowledge they never even talked about it. They managed our finances extremely well. I entrusted our executive pastor to represent me, which he did superbly. He knew my convictions and my commitments, and he knew my pragmatic sensibilities, and he represented those, too. But that took years of building trust and understanding. You don't do that in year one. I was there for 20 years, and we went through a relocation and a building, so we had plenty of opportunity to exercise those commitments, those convictions, and those pragmatic decisions so that we learned to trust each other. I knew I didn't need to be there unless they asked me to be there for some specific reason.

Be Clear

You also need to be clear about expectations. Talk to them about the way you want church members treated. Talk to them about the way you expect them to walk closely with the Lord. Do not assume staff members know these things. Talk to them about how you want them to treat women with respect, how you want them to practice godly relationships, handle money, and live blamelessly. Make that a priority and something you talk about frequently. When you're clear about expectations, then you can hold them accountable. But frankly, when you have good people on staff, and you're clear in expectations, people usually live up or down to your expectations. Set the bar high. Live to it yourself. Don't ask them to do what you're not doing. Model what you expect from them, and empower them to act on your behalf. Don't always look over somebody's shoulder when you delegate a job. Once I entrust a task to someone, we only need to talk if they need my counsel or if they're not following through on the job.

Be Encouraging

God has blessed me with wonderful people around me in ministry. The men and women who work around me at Southern Seminary and Buck Run Baptist Church are amazing. I do my best to be clear in my expectations, and they're clear in the way they do them because they're empowered, and I trust them. Trust is an important part of any relationship. They must be able to trust you. You need to be able to trust them. If you don't, there's a problem and you need to figure that out because you simply can't work alongside someone very long if you don't trust them.

Encourage them. Thank them. It's just a part of a pastor's vocabulary to say, "Thank you for doing that." That is food for their souls to hear you say thank you. And I noticed when you catch people doing things right, they do more right things. You always reproduce whatever you honor. So, honor them for doing their job well. And this makes them want to continue to do the right thing.

Years ago, I heard a preacher say you need to give ten "atta-boys" for every one "you jerk." Though I came to believe it's probably twice that, his point was that people need praise a lot more than they need correction. There's a lot of fussing in the world already, and they're getting fussed at by other people. I want to encourage them. I'm certainly going to be honest with them. If I think something wasn't helpful, I'm going to explain why it wasn't. But if it's in doubt, we're going to talk about it. I'll ask why they did it, and we're going to be clear.

Another key principle is to put their needs before your own. I tell all the people working with me that I am glad they work here and hope they stay here a long time. But if they ever say this isn't working out, this isn't really what they want to do, or they would like to look for another place or job, they don't have to hide that from me. I will help them find the place of service they want. I'm their guy. Unless they've done something disreputable or dishonorable, I'm going to help them find a place of service. Even if I don't want them to go, and even if it hurts me to lose them, I'll have that conversation and assure them of my assistance and blessing.

Also, never penalize somebody for doing a good job. If someone has done a great job in their position, but they want to move up or move on, I don't hold them back because they were successful and I don't want to lose them. If you look at the history of the pastors who've served with me at Buck Run, many of them came in as interns, got a permanent position, and then went from a permanent position to a pastoral one. They showed a propensity for that, and I wanted to empower them to fulfill their calling. If they come to you and tell you of a position open in another state that they'd like to be considered for, don't be hurt. Don't be wounded. Be their defender. Be their advocate and say, "If that's what you want to do, then I'm going to help you do that."

In the future, people who come to work for you will talk to the people who used to work for you. Live so they all can testify you treated them well with honor and respect. That helps you do your job. And when you treat people that way, you're working together, you're pastoring together, you're shepherding together; and it helps you pastor well.

11

How Should I Respond When Others Disappoint Me?

When people hurt you, how do you love them? How do you let them leave? Well, unfortunately, that's going to happen a lot through the years. Remember that Peter said in 1 Peter 5:1 to "shepherd the flock of God that is among you." Now, that verse says a lot, and one of the things it says is to not spend your time shepherding somebody else's flock or the flock you wish you had or the flock you hope you one day get or even the flock you used to have. Don't spend all your time on the internet looking at someone else's ministry and thinking, "Boy, I wish I had that." Shepherd your flock.

But you cannot walk through life with your flock without people sometimes letting you down and disappointing you. They're going to hurt you. You will find that sometimes the people you seem to have the best fellowship with will then use their closeness with you to wound you. I've had it happen. I've seen it happen to others many times. How do you deal with that?

Hope in the Lord, Not in Sinners

Well, begin by reminding yourself that your hope is in the Lord. Your hope is not in people. People are broken and fallen, and people often respond to you based on other things in their lives. They're broken by other situations. Maybe some other pastor hurt them, and it comes out on you. They are also sinners, and sinners hurt others. Psalm 55 says "It was not my enemy that reproached me, for then I could have borne it.

It was you, my brother." The Lord Jesus himself had to deal with that. Judas betrayed him. Simon Peter denied him. You and I will also be hurt, betrayed, and denied by people we love.

Don't Let Them Smell Anger

How can we respond? The key is to never let them smell fear or anger on you. The pastor cannot afford to show those two emotions. Now you can feel all of that you want. Feelings are neither good nor bad, right nor wrong. The issue is always what you do with those feelings. It's going to hurt when someone betrays you, but you can't act out of your hurt and woundedness. You can't go around moping and dragging. You can't act angry and vengeful. You must be able to keep your cool, and, if at all possible, you want to meet with the person and show them grace and forgiveness.

Confront Them with Humility

If someone lashes out or has turned on you, it's appropriate to find out from them why they did what they did or why they're upset. Is it something you did? Try to understand. But when you speak to them, you must be unemotional in your affect. You can't be angry, wounded, or vengeful. Approach them with humility and love.

Often, when you confront people, they repent. In fact, that should be your expectation and hope. In my experience, that happens more often than not. When you meet with someone when there's a breach between you, but you approach them with humility and grace, it really can often be resolved in that meeting. There's just something about Christians coming together, beginning with prayer, and seeking the Lord. The Lord can really use these events because it establishes a pattern in the church that the pastor is going to come talk to someone and seek to resolve things. People begin to expect that it's not acceptable or normal for divisions to be left smoldering below the surface. If something is between you and some church members, you cannot simply ignore it.

If They Don't Like You

But let's say you go talk to somebody, and they have no confidence in you. They don't like you, and they don't like what you're doing. Maybe they used to be friends, but now they're done with you, and they say they are leaving the church. How do you deal with that?

Make it your goal to let them leave as friends unless they are overtly trying to cause division and convince others to leave with them. Then, you must make sure other people understand what's going on and have to go into a bit more of a defensive posture when people intentionally try to wound the church. Fortunately, most people don't do that. Most people just say they are leaving, or they simply disappear. What do you do? You need to talk with them if possible, and write a letter if meeting with them proves impossible. Tell them you are sorry that you will no longer be their pastor but let them know you will always remain their friend and brother in Christ. If you run into each other at the grocery store, you don't want there to be a minute of awkwardness. Express gratitude for all they have done for the church while they were here, and make sure they know they go with your thanks for their investment. Pray that God might bless them and use them for his glory.

Keep the Door Open

Also remind them that, if they find things aren't really what they thought they were at some other place, that the door swings in both directions, and you hope one day they will come back. Here is something remarkable. If you can bring yourself to say that, you will be shocked how frequently people will end up coming back because they don't find elsewhere the expositional preaching that you do or the kind of fellowship that they enjoyed at your church. They're going to discover that other churches have problems too, and maybe they've got bigger problems than you have, and if you let them leave well and without rancor, they return much happier and more committed than ever.

Sometimes, people just leave. There are people sometimes who leave who I thought needed to leave. Maybe they weren't happy or weren't letting others be happy and they needed to go somewhere where they could be happy. I'll write a letter, if I didn't have a meeting with them, that tells them I love them. I've had people who left and joined another church, and within a year, they were back. They learned a lesson, and they came home more on my team than they ever were when they left. So love on them and keep the door open, keep your heart open, and show no negative emotion toward them.

Sometimes it's going to hurt. Control your emotions. Be loving. Remember, they're not your sheep. They're God's sheep. Let them go. Encourage them. Bless them. The Lord will use that in your leadership and in the people who are with you because they can say their pastor handles that kind of thing well. It gives them greater confidence in your leadership and might also gain your brother back as well. Whether they return or not, honor the Lord by the way you treat them. When you do that, you pastor well.

12

How Should I Respond When I Disappoint Others?

In the previous chapter, I dealt with what to do when others disappoint you and how you should let them leave. Now, I want to address what happens when you disappoint others. You're not always going to do things right or do things well. You're not always going to pastor well. So what happens when you pastor badly? When people let you know that you messed up and hurt them? Several reasons can lead to people being disappointed in you.

You Will Blow It

The most obvious one is because of what you've done. Pastors can blow it. Pastors can do things badly. Sometimes, pastors take for themselves an authority that's not theirs. They unilaterally make decisions that weren't theirs to make. They slay sacred cows that weren't ready to be slain, and people don't like it. You didn't consult with them; you didn't talk to them. Maybe you just ran roughshod over their feelings. When you do these kinds of wrong things, people will let you know because you hurt them.

The second reason that you can disappoint people is because of what you didn't do. Now, in my own life in ministry, I will tell you this is probably ten to one of what I hear. People get disappointed in me more because of what I did not do that they thought I should do, instead of something I did wrong. There's a unique challenge in ministry: our people expect us to be proactive, realize that something needs to be done, and then do it, whether or not anyone informs us about the problem. No one, if they get into a legal problem, expects their lawyer to just know it and to call them. If someone gets sick, they don't expect their doctor to call them. But when people get into a spiritual issue, they expect their pastor to be proactive, hear about it, and show up. You can disappoint people by not showing up when they think you should, not showing the kindness that they expected you to show, or failing to display excitement at something that happened to them.

I served as pastor of Buck Run for 20 years, and all that time, I only had one deacons' meeting that had any tension in it, and I'm the guy who brought the tension in the room because I went into the meeting anticipating that there was a course of action we had to take and only one way to do it. I'd already thought through every permutation of the matter that I could think of, and I knew I had to make a decision. I knew some people wouldn't like the decision, and I set myself up to be upset. And sure enough, when I told them of this decision, I really wanted them to just get on board.

I had two very godly, wonderful deacons who said, "Wait just a minute, you're wanting our approval of this decision, but we are just hearing this for the first time, and we think we ought to have a little bit of time to think about this and pray about this." I had told myself that somebody was going to do that. I came back at them. I didn't say these words, but let's just say it was the "how dare you question me" kind of thing, which is a terrible posture for a pastor to show. And I showed it. I had to apologize to those deacons privately. And then, at the next deacons' meeting, I apologized to them again in front of all the deacons. I disappointed them. When you fail, you simply need to own it.

Own It

A church should never be shocked to hear their pastor say, "I'm sorry." Some people never expect apologies from certain individuals, but I don't want to be that kind of person. That's just not what a New Testament Christian is. We all fail. We are all broken. And when I legitimately fail to live up to my own standards, let alone to someone else's, I want to be quick to apologize and say, "I just blew that. Can you forgive me?" People are usually happy to forgive you. They just want to know that you know you did wrong. They're not expecting a perfect pastor, but they do expect their pastor to know when he's messed up and to own it. They will love you more for it. But if you deny it, you're going into defensive mode. You need to be willing to own your mistakes, ask their forgiveness, and thank them for pointing it out.

Sometimes, people are going to be disappointed in you because of unreasonable expectations. Let's say they send an anonymous letter. Should you read an anonymous letter? Well, unless you have someone designated to read your mail, you probably will. It's hard not to read them. People find a way to make sure you get them. The question is, when you get one, is it a legitimate gripe? Is there a legitimate cause for complaint? You need to consider that. Is there something you need to adjust? Now, you've got nobody to apologize to because you don't know who the person is. I would advise you not to mention to your congregation that you received an anonymous letter. I think that empowers the anonymous letter writers. That's the moment they're going for. Don't give it to them. Just deal with the issue if it needs to be dealt with. And if they write an unreasonable expectation in that letter, throw it in the trash, and do your best to forget it. But if they say something like "you preach too long", look back at the record. How long do you preach? Have you been getting longer? Is this an unreasonable expectation? We can all defend ourselves and say, "If they loved Jesus, they should be happy to sit there for an hour and five minutes!" You have to be an unusually good preacher to hold people for an hour and five minutes. So maybe you do need to cut that back. You don't need to make a big announcement about it. Just consider whether the anonymous complaint is legitimate or not. If it's not, ignore it.

When people see that you're willing to own your mistakes, that you want to grow from them, that you're not just venting, and you're not defensive, over time people respond well to that kind of humility. Humility is such a key aspect, not only in the Christian life, but in any godly pastor. We need to show it. So when you disappoint them, if you need to own it, then own it. If you need to ask forgiveness, do so. They'll see that you're serious about serving the Lord, and that will help you pastor well.

13

Is a Pastor-Led Church or an Elder-Led Church Better?

What is more biblical — a pastor-led model of church polity or an elder-led model? Well, this is a great question, and there's a lot of discussion about it, but my answer is within my convictions. Remember, I'm a professor at The Southern *Baptist* Theological Seminary. Historically, baptists are convictionally congregational. Therefore, I'm ruling out the possibility of elder rule. Elder rule is not a baptist model because baptists are congregational. We believe that churches are congregational in their government, but what's the best way to lead a congregationally governed church? Is it through a single lead pastor or a group of pastors called elders?

The Pastorate in the New Testament

The answer is really not as simple as you might suppose. First, let's just look at what the New Testament says. Baptists have always understood the three titles for the office of the pastorate in the New Testament — *poimen*, the word for pastor or shepherd, *episkopos*, which is the word translated bishop or overseer, and *presbuteros*, usually translated elder — as a single office. So, whether we speak of a pastor, an overseer, or an elder, we are talking about one and the same office. To say that there's either a pastor-led or an elder-led church, really, in one sense, is to say the same thing because they refer to the same office. It gets down to whether you believe in a single pastor who is leading the congregation and perhaps other pastors, or do you believe in a group of pastors all with an equal voice?

What Works Best

Before I answer the question, I remind you that I am convictional — I don't compromise my convictions for convenience's sake — but I'm also a pragmatist within my convictions. In other words, if the Bible does not narrowly specify something, and within that scriptural truth you have room for multiple views, then I'm going to ask what works best. I believe that church polity or church governance falls into that category. There's clear teaching about the church and its offices, but it also leaves quite a bit of space for how they function. For instance, I believe it is clear that the churches in the New Testament have a pastoral leader and sometimes more than one leader, but you seem to see one dominant leader — for instance, in the church of Jerusalem. When the council at Jerusalem takes place, many of them discuss the matters at hand, but then James seems to be the leader, and when James speaks it ends the matter.

The pastoral epistles indicate both a plurality of elders, yet at the same time when Paul writes to young Timothy, he's writing to teach Timothy how to lead the Church of God. He's not addressing that to a group of elders. He's writing it to one. The same thing is true with the book of Titus. Even though Paul tells Titus to appoint elders in every city, the fact that he's telling Titus to do it means that he's invested this one man with the authority to appoint others. But at the same time, there is clearly a plurality evident when Paul talks to the Ephesian elders in Acts 20. A group of men from the church at Ephesus come to see him on his journey, and he addresses them as elders.

In 1 Peter 5, Peter says, "I who am a fellow elder and a witness of the sufferings of Christ and the glory that will be revealed to you, exhort the elders among you to shepherd the flock of God which is among you, exercising oversight." In that passage, Peter uses some form of all three of those words for the office of pastor. He's writing to a plural group of elders. But that doesn't really solve the issue because it's a group of churches. If you read the beginning of the epistle, Peter addresses not a single church but a group of churches scattered throughout that part of the world because of the persecution, and we don't know whether he's writing to a plural group of elders for each church or just all the different elders of the different churches.

It's also not clear in the Book of Revelation that every church has multiple elders on equal terms. You have Jesus addressing the letters to the seven churches through the Apostle John, and he speaks to the seven churches, which are the seven lampstands. But then he holds also in his hand the seven stars of the seven churches, which he says are the angels or messengers of those churches. And the most accepted view traditionally is that those are the pastors of those seven churches. In that case, you would have one key man serving as the pastor — the angel, if you will, the messenger of that church. So frankly, I do not believe there is only one option and all others are unscriptural. In my experience what works best in a congregational government is that one key leader is responsible as the pastor-teacher to open the Word and proclaim the Word.

Now, I don't think it's wrong for a church where you have multiple men who share that duty. I don't think it's a matter of right and wrong. I think it's a matter of pragmatism. What works best in that church and in that particular culture? I grew up in the model in which a single man served as a pastor, and maybe he had other pastors around him who served as staff and additional pastors, but he served as the key leader. He served as the one who was the pastor-teacher, and the understanding was that he would stand before the Lord and answer for the direction of the church and the spiritual leadership of that church in a way greater than the others would. On the other hand I have seen churches function extremely well with a plurality of elders who had equal authority. But on the other hand, I have seen both models fail miserably, too. Our depravity can show itself whatever the model.

The Need for Accountability

In the two churches I pastored for many years, we had a plurality of pastors, but the others all served under my authority as the Senior Pastor. At Buck Run we had seven pastors. You might wonder: How does that work? How does that function? A lot of people asked the other guys who held me accountable, and the answer to that question was "everybody." I met with our deacons monthly, and I reported to them (there were 39 of them), and they were free to raise anything or ask any question. They were not my bosses, but they were definitely key men in the church who had the respect of the congregation. And I learned to trust them as they trusted me. I ran ideas by them as I did with our other pastors.

I didn't do anything autocratically. If I couldn't build a consensus with my other pastors, I didn't feel comfortable to move forward with anything. There's no scenario in which my other pastors didn't like an idea, but I just didn't care and moved ahead. That just didn't happen. And I think it's a very good model. I had wise counsel around me, and I had the freedom and the responsibility to lead. Even though I very much like the model in which I served, I would never say that a plurality of elders in which each of them has an equal say is a bad model. Again, my personal preference and belief is that what is most pragmatic, what works best, is when you have a key leader who influences others and has a significant amount of authority but not autocratic authority.

Now, sometimes people object and say it's easy for a pastor to fail morally in that kind of polity. I'm just going to say I've been in ministry and around churches and pastors for a long time, and I don't think there are any shortcuts around depravity. I probably see failures in churches that have a plurality of elders at about the same rate. We all need accountability. We all need to be able to explain ourselves and why we make the decisions we make. But I do think what you see in Scripture is that key leader — the pastor, teacher, the star in the hand of Jesus, if you will, the messenger of the church as you see in Revelation — and that he has a key role. When people start attending a church, it's harder for them to identify with multiple voices in the pulpit than it is one key leader. And, ironically, in the churches that purport to have an elder-led model of polity, I still usually see one key leader. It's hard to imagine that a pastor who has preached in a pulpit for decades is not going to have more influence with the congregation or that men half his age would not defer to him on most matters.

As a young preacher of about 28, I was in the room one time when Adrian Rogers and John MacArthur were having this friendly debate. Adrian represented the key leader model, and John MacArthur represented an elder-led model. MacArthur was trying to convince

Adrian that he should have a plurality of elders. Adrian argued that he did that. He responded that all of the pastors on his staff were elders. They all met the qualifications of pastor. MacArthur said that was not the same. And then Adrian said, "Now, John, are you telling me that there's something in Grace Community Church that you want to do and it does not happen?" MacArthur just sort of grinned at that. It was a telling moment because there were two very, very strong leaders, both claiming to be in a little bit different kind of polity, and yet both clearly the leaders in their churches. And I don't think MacArthur's authority or influence in his church has declined through the decades since!

Conclusion

Here is the crux of what I'm saying: a man of God who lives according to the biblical qualifications, is transparent in his leadership, who candidly shares his reasoning and the basis of his leadership with other pastors and leaders and is the person who stands before the congregation week in and week out with a Bible open, faithfully teaching the Word of God, is going to have a lot of trust and influence regardless of how many elders you put around him. People are listening for a shepherd's voice. So, it's healthy and necessary for there to be transparency and accountability. Whoever is opening the Word of God and teaching the Word of God is the person who will most easily earn the leadership credibility in that church. But whoever a church installs in that role and bestows that title upon should meet all the qualifications of being an elder or a pastor. That means he must meet the moral qualifications and the requirement of being a fit teacher, as well as the right kind of leader in his home. Whether it's the person standing up there in front of the congregation or a paid pastor or a lay elder. If a church uses any pastoral title, the church is attesting that this pastor has the function and meets all the biblical qualifications and requirements.

I think the New Testament leaves a lot of leeway for pastoral structures. There's no clear single model to follow. And I do think some expression of this is cultural, but it must always be biblical first of all. We want to emulate that. We want to be accountable, and we certainly want to be godly in all our fulfillment of it. But whatever our role, whether we're the teaching pastor or in some other elder role in the church, we need to meet all the qualifications, and we need to do it within the anointing and power of the Holy Spirit. And when we do that, we will pastor well.

PART 4

Shepherd Well

The Pastor and His Flock

14

When Is a Child Ready to Be Baptized?

Can a child really know Jesus Christ as Lord and Savior? If so, should we baptize children? Let me begin by saying, I'm not talking about baptizing infants who have not yet professed their faith in Christ. I am thoroughly a baptist, and that means I'm a credobaptist. I believe in baptizing only those who have made a credible profession of faith in the Lord Jesus Christ. That means they've repented of their sins, and they have called on the name of the Lord for salvation and confessed Jesus as Lord. They are willing to join a New Testament church and be discipled. And I believe baptism is the first act of obedience of a believer. So, can a child be saved and baptized and be a church member? Well, let's divide the question.

Can a Child Be Saved?

I believe the Bible teaches that children can have faith. Faith occurs when a child realizes they are a sinner, are separated from God by their sin, and are lost apart from his grace. They realize they must put their faith and trust in Jesus, understanding that he died on the cross in their place, rose from the grave, reigns in heaven, and is coming back.

A child needs to understand who Jesus is and what he did to save us. A child has to understand the gospel. But more than understanding the facts of the gospel, there has to be a personal commitment. Now, do I think it's possible? Well, I know it's possible. How do I know it? I did it. When I was five years old, I came under conviction of my sin. I can remember the very night I came under conviction of my sin and a terrible weight. A burden descended upon me, and it remained there for over a year. From sometime when I was five until I had just turned seven, I labored under the knowledge of my sin. I can remember going to church on Sundays, my knuckles gripping the pew, fearing I was going to just drop into hell. My dad was not one of the guys that just talked about hell all the time. He did preach wrath, and he preached hell, but he was a grace preacher, and he offered salvation.

But I knew I was separated from God, and that just weighed me down. And knowing that I was a sinner, that if I died in that condition, I would be lost — it gripped my heart for over a year. And I can remember the very night (it was just a few days after I turned seven on a Sunday night) my dad preached, and I do not recall precisely what he preached, but in reality, it wasn't about what he preached that night. This had been a process, and I had been thinking about the gospel and knowing I had to repent. And that night, I came to absolutely rest in Christ. There's no other way to put it. I just said, "Lord, I can't get this off of me. I can't do anything about my sin. Will you take it? Will you forgive me? I receive you as Lord and Savior." I just broke, and it was like, immediately, that weight was lifted. I remember we had a hymn of invitation at the end of the service, and I went forward and, through tears, told my dad that I had trusted Christ. The next week I was baptized. I'm 63 years old. I can tell you, in all honesty, that there's not been a time in my life where I looked back on that event and questioned whether it really happened, whether or not it was genuine, whether or not I was saved.

When I was a freshman in college, I went through a few months of intellectual doubts, and I very quickly reached a point where I said, either the Bible is completely true or it's not trustworthy. I could not accept anything in between. I realized that if Jesus really rose from the dead, everything else is secondary to that. Everything else is true. And if Jesus didn't rise from the dead, nothing else matters. And it was really that experience as a 7-year-old that I knew God saved me. Then as a freshman at Michigan State University, I responded to the Lord's call to serve him in ministry knowing that, whatever he asked of me, I would do. And I've never questioned the reality of that. Those intellectual doubts didn't last very long. I just had to come face to face with whether I believed what I believed because they were my dad's convictions or whether or not they were really my convictions. I knew that the faith I had as a 7-year-old was the faith God gave me to face those doubts. I've never questioned it. Now, yes, I have known other people who told me that they made professions of faith as a child, and later, looking back on it, they said it wasn't real. But frankly, I've known adults who said that about their adult profession of faith.

What I have learned is when I talk to a child to understand their attitude about sin, sometimes parents will bring a child to me, and I'll talk to them, and they'll say something like this, "I want to be baptized because I love Jesus. I want to go to heaven when I die." And they just express this general desire to follow the God of their parents, the God they hear about in Sunday School. I will say to their parents, "I think Susie here is taking a step toward Christ. I think God's clearly at work. She somewhat understands what is involved in salvation, but I don't think she's there yet. Let's just give her time to process this. Let's let the Holy Spirit do his work. I really do believe he who began a good work will complete it. We don't need to pressure or rush anything. Let's just let her continue this journey of faith, and I think the Holy Spirit will make it clear." But when a child comes in and says they know they are a sinner and they know they can't save themselves, and they have put faith in Jesus Christ or be lost, that's the attitude towards sin that makes me know they are serious about it.

Don't Turn Them Away

Jesus said, "Allow the little children to come to me." He said that to be his follower, we had to become like little children. He did not say that little children have to become like adults. So, I believe that a child can understand enough. They can understand their lostness and their sinfulness, and they can understand that Jesus died in their place, that God raised him from the dead, and they can understand that he loves them, and they can respond in love to him. If they do that, then I think nothing should hinder them from being baptized.

I know there are godly Christian people whom I love and respect who say we should wait and observe children before baptism, but I don't see in the New Testament any waiting period that's prescribed for anybody. When a person repents and believes, they're baptized. We certainly must have the highest integrity in our evangelism methods. I don't believe in putting any pressure on a child (or an adult, for that matter). I don't believe in any psychological arm-twisting to get them to make a profession. I don't believe in telling them it's time they made a profession. Nothing like that. I believe in letting the Holy Spirit do his work. But if a child expresses repentance and faith, I think they are ready to be baptized. I'm grateful I was saved as a 7-year-old instead of as a 27-year-old. I think about what God protected me from and what he spared me from because I knew him and because I had the Holy Spirit in my heart and in my life. Do nothing to compel a child, do nothing to pressure a child, but let them come to Jesus.

Are Baptized Children Full Members?

And if they come to Jesus, I think it's proper to baptize them. The New Testament pattern — without exception — is that someone believed and was baptized. There may be legitimate questions about church membership that come up. Does that mean they're full members of a church? Well, a baptist church can establish their own rules of membership. Now, personally, I believe that when a person is baptized, they're baptized by a church into the fellowship of that church. It's a church ordinance. That's what the Baptist Faith and Message says. So I do believe that anybody, child or adult, who makes a profession of faith and is baptized is baptized into membership.

It's not improper, however, for a church to say there are certain privileges of membership, like voting, that are available only to adults. That certainly does not violate any Scriptural principle. But even though a child may be limited in participation in church governance, a believing child should be able to be baptized upon their profession of faith and then participate in the Lord's Supper as an ongoing testimony and memorial of what Christ did and of their own profession of faith. Part of a pastor's job is to disciple them, to teach them, and to train them. But it is far better to bring them up in the nurture and the admonition of the Lord as believers than to refuse them access to Christ and obedience to his command.

Nowhere in scripture are we commanded to tell them, "No, this is not for you. You can't do this."

Let Them Follow Jesus

We should lovingly and carefully teach children the gospel and then allow the Holy Spirit to do his work. When the fruit is ripe, it will fall from the tree. That is the work of the Spirit. And let's let the Holy Spirit lead them and give voice to their profession. Let's let them follow Jesus in baptism and then in discipleship. I think this is one of the healthiest things that churches can do in bringing up the next generation so that even as children, they are taught to love the Word of God, to follow the prompting of the Holy Spirit through the Word, and to follow Christ. And part of being a shepherd is to help children do that as the Holy Spirit leads them. That's part of pastoring well.

15

How Should I Practice Church Discipline?

One of the most difficult issues a pastor can face is church discipline. How do we practice church discipline? The better question, I think, is how do you teach it? How do you implement it? Because you will not practice church discipline if you're only reacting to situations that have already occurred. You need to teach church discipline before a situation arises, if at all possible, early in your ministry. In any church, you need to make sure you teach it before you are in a crisis.

Teach the Scriptural Basis

Now, the classic text on this doctrine is Matthew 18. Isn't it interesting that Jesus only used the word *ecclesia*, the word for church, three times in all the Gospels, and all three are in Matthew? Matthew 16, when he says, upon this rock I'll build my *ecclesia*, my church, and the gates of hell will not prevail against it. Then in Matthew 18, the next time he mentions it, it's in the context of church discipline. If you've got something against your brother, you go to him, and then if he won't hear you, go back with two or three others. If he won't hear you, then you tell the church, and then if he won't hear the church, you put him out of the church. It's fascinating that two of the three times Jesus used the word were related to church discipline. That is certainly an indication of the significance of this doctrine.

First of all, I believe that the church was established during the earthly ministry of Jesus. It makes no sense that he was talking about discipline for something that didn't yet exist. So, the church is empowered at the Pentecost, but I don't think it was born then. I think it's spoken into existence in Matthew 16, and his disciples are his incipient church. By the day of Pentecost, the number is 120, and then 3,000 added to it after that outpouring of the Holy Spirit. The point is that there are a number, and they know who's in and who's not. Jesus is telling them what to do with the person who is in the church but living as though he were not.

The other classic church discipline test, of course, is 1 Corinthians 5, where Paul addresses the issue of the man who was having sex with his stepmother. In that chapter, Paul deals with that four times, in four different ways, explicitly telling them that they must put that man out of the church.

Now, here is what I want to encourage pastors to do. You need to teach your church that sin is always harmful, that the cruelest thing you can do is leave someone in sin, and the kindest thing you can do is to do everything possible to get them out of sin. What's the number one objection to church discipline you hear in churches? People say, "Oh, who are we to judge? The Bible says, judge not." Well, in the very chapter in Matthew 7 where Jesus said, "judge not," just down a few verses, he says, "Don't cast your pearls before swine. Don't give that which is holy to the dogs." Clearly, Jesus is saying that some people are spiritual swine and spiritual dogs, which requires judgment. Therefore, when Jesus said, "Judge not, that you be not judged," he was not saying have no judgment. He was telling us to judge with *righteous* judgment and judge according to the Word.

You're always going to have to deal with people's fear. The fear that many church members express is "If we believe in discipline, doesn't that make us self-righteous?" They fear that if you teach what the Bible actually says, some bad thing will happen. You need to show people that the bad thing that will happen is that the people in sin will *stay* in sin. The whole point of church discipline is *always* restoration.

Teach Restoration

Your goal is to restore them. "Go to your brother," Jesus said. Why? So that you can regain your brother. If he won't hear you, you go back to him. Why? Because you still want to regain him. If he doesn't hear the two or three, then you tell it to the church. Why? Well, Paul says in 1 Corinthians 5 that even when you put him out of the church, you put him out of the church so that his spirit may be saved in the day of Christ Jesus. On the day of judgment, you want him to be saved. If you let him live in sin, you assume that he's lost, and that means he's going to die and go to hell. If you don't confront people in their sins, you are literally saying to them that they can go to hell.

When you care about your people so much that you're willing to go to them and plead with them to forsake their sins, repent, and return, you're showing real care, and that's the way you must teach it. My sermon on church discipline is called "The Compassion of Confrontation." That's precisely the way I teach it. I have many, many stories throughout a lifetime of ministry. I could tell you about so many times when people were confronted, and they repented. In fact, my experience is that they repented most of the time. Sometimes they will not repent, and then I pray for them, and maybe later they will. But I'll tell you this: people who you ignore and leave in sin don't tend to repent. You've got to go to them and beg them to repent.

Now, what's the process? First, not every sin rises to the level of church discipline. The Bible teaches three that do. There's the sin of gross immorality. Paul says in 1 Corinthians 5 that there's a guy who does what even the Gentiles don't do. Even the Gentiles know that that's wrong. And in this case, it was a man having sex with his stepmother. There's also the case of doctrinal heresy. In Romans 16:17-20, Paul says those that teach contrary to the faith of Jesus Christ must be dealt with. Then, in Titus 3:9-10 he warns against those who are intentionally divisive, those who are sowing discord in the church, and even when admonished, they just keep it up. They don't care about the unity of the church, and they have no spirit of working together. If they won't repent, then you put them out. So those three things rise to the level of church discipline. The fourth category is the sin of an elder. When an elder sins, the Bible says to rebuke him before all so others may fear (1 Tim 5:21). When an elder falls into serious sin, he must be publicly corrected even though removed from his office.

Let me give an example. Imagine that two church members move in together as husband and wife even though they are not married. Now, this is clearly wrong and against the Word of God. When I faced this in the church, I had to confront them, call on them to repent, and tell them why what they were doing was wrong. If they won't repent, we will go back to them again. And then, if they still won't, we tell that to the church in a member's meeting and ask the church to remove them from fellowship because they won't repent. But when we do that, we always record in the record that we do this with tears in the hope of their eventual repentance and return so that they can be restored.

If someone is disciplined, they've been removed from the roll of the church, and we ask them to go through a restoration process when they come back. We would surround them with a group of people around them that disciple them. It's like starting all over in some ways. After a while of teaching and observing, that group around them will declare them restored to full fellowship, provided they do what they are asked to do. The goal is always to restore them. When we remove someone, we may not hear from them for years, but we still pray they'll return.

If you tell your people that the motive of church discipline is always restoration, they are much more likely to follow you in discipline because they see that it's not being judgmental and that it's truly caring and aimed towards delivering them. It's one of the hardest things that a pastor will do. But it's also one of the most important things because your people will see the beauty of repentance and restoration.

Conclusion

Satan will try to make you fear this. Admittedly, it's hard to implement discipline in a church that has never seen it, but once they see it work, everything changes. Someone very close to me who once was disciplined told me he knows that church discipline saved his life. I've heard that from several people throughout the years. Their testimony is not just that it restored them, but it saved their lives. They think they would've gone off into sin and even death. So, you have the compassion to confront people in their sin and remove them from the church if necessary, but always in hopes that they'll return in repentance. Always give them a clear path of repentance. Tell them what they need to do to be restored and pray for them toward that end. By practicing church discipline, you're teaching a church to uphold the standards of the gospel, to be obedient. And indeed, this will help you pastor well.

16

How Should I Minister to Those with Same-Sex Attraction?

Ministering to same-sex attracted people in our churches is one of the most difficult issues evangelical pastors today will face. Now, to be clear, I am not talking about those who are pursuing a behavior that is outside of Scripture and outside the will of God and who do not care what Scripture says. I am talking about those people in your church who want to honor the Lord, and yet they come to you and tell you that they are attracted to members of the same sex. Pastors will encounter people who want to honor the Lord and are willing to live a celibate lifestyle or maybe even people who are married but feel attraction to members of the same sex. When people come to you with these challenges, pastors who believe the Word of God need to be able to deal with that issue biblically, sensitively, helpfully, and in a way that is consistent with Scripture that will encourage that person to follow Christ.

Fallen, Not Special

One of the first principles that I express to same-sex attracted people is, first of all, that I appreciate the fact they feel comfortable telling me because I realize it is a very personal thing, and some people immediately feel like they will be attacked or criticized for simply feeling the temptation. Next, I also share with them that even feeling that temptation is a result of fallenness. In other words, it is an inherently disordered desire. It is not a desire Adam and Eve would've felt before the fall, and I do not think it would've been possible for them to feel same-sex attraction if anybody of the same sex were there. That's something that happened after the fall. We are in a fallen world that is inherently disordered, so we shouldn't be shocked when someone feels this and expresses it. We need to be candid with them and say that the temptation they feel is something that Satan wants to use to cause them to fall away from God. He wants them to value their disordered desire more than their desire to follow Christ.

On one level, I always explain to same-sex attracted people that they are not special. They shouldn't think for a moment that their struggle is somehow harder than a heterosexual person who is trying to live a celibate lifestyle and go through life single. This is simply their struggle, and they have got to lay this at the foot of Jesus and say, "Lord, I need you to help me defeat this." So, encourage them that, on one level, this is everyone's struggle in some way, that we all struggle with our sexuality because our sexuality, like every other part of our being, is fallen. Though someone else may not feel same-sex attraction, they still feel the temptation of sexual desire outside of the boundaries that God has given for it to be expressed.

What Do You Desire More?

I always explain to people they must ask themselves what it is that they want more. Do you want to satisfy the desires of your flesh more or do you want to honor Jesus more? One evidence of genuine salvation is that you want to honor the Lord more. It doesn't mean you don't feel temptation, but what you want is to follow Christ. I mean, if there were a button that you could push that would take that away, wouldn't you push it? If I could push a button that took away all temptation so that I could follow Christ without feeling any temptation whatsoever of any kind, I'd push it. Because what I want more than anything is to honor and follow him. So, our desire to honor Christ is evidence of our salvation.

It is wrong for a pastor to assume, believe, or teach that if you really are saved, then you just automatically lose that desire. I don't think that's realistic. We wouldn't say that to a person who is attracted to the opposite sex. Any married person can still feel sexual desires toward someone else. The issue is not whether you feel it. The issue is what you do with it.

And this is where, by the power of the Holy Spirit, we yield ourselves to the will of God, to the indwelling Christ, and to the power of the Holy Spirit. Over and over, especially in Paul's epistles, Scripture emphasizes our mind and the way we think. In Romans 8, we are to be minding the things of the spirit, not the things of the flesh. And he tells us in Philippians, whatever things are true and lovely and honest and of good reputation, think on these things.

We are told to bring every thought captive to Christ. And so much of the Christian life is understanding who we are in Christ and then acting like it. I think you can sort of summarize all the ethical teachings of Paul's epistles in this one sentence: act like what you are. And that's true for any Christian. We have the temptation to act like what we were instead of like who Jesus says we are. We were crucified with Christ. We have risen with Christ. We are seated with him in the heavenly places. We are indwelled by the Holy Spirit. So much of defeating temptation is reminding ourselves of who we are, that we died with Christ, we're dead to sin, and we're raised to walk in a new way of life. Sin has no more power over us. But it's not that this magically takes place, and desire is erased with temptation gone. I don't know anybody like that. I'm certainly not like that. I feel temptation of all kinds, whether it's my pride, my anger, greed, or any number of things. Whatever the temptation, the response must be the same thing — I want Christ more. I want to think on the things of the spirit, not on the things of the flesh.

Encourage Them to Follow Christ

If a person comes to me with same-sex attraction, I want to encourage them to continue to pursue Christ. Some say they will never be attracted to a person of the opposite sex, but they are willing to live a celibate lifestyle to honor Christ. They want you to help them do that. Well, one of the things that you need to help your church do is make sure that families include singles, and singles of all kinds, in your church, in their homes. When you go on a day trip to a museum or something, invite a single person to come with you, and include single people in your life. In our community groups, we don't just have a community group for married people and another group of single people. We want people of all kinds — young, old, married, single, and widowed — in the same community groups because that is community life, and they all need each other. They all need to contribute to each other. They need to hear from one another. And so, I would encourage same-sex attracted people to be around couples, to be around families in the same way that I would encourage families to reach out to the singles in your congregation because what we're doing is provoking one another to love and good works.

I tell same-sex attracted people what a blessing it is to hear them say they want to follow Christ. This is true no matter what the temptation or the background of any member of my church. That's what the church is here for and what we want to do. I want to get them in the Scripture. I want to get them in prayer, in community groups and accountability groups. I want our church to minister to them. Again, they're not special. They're not the only ones facing temptation. But we need to be prepared and compassionate because I don't think it's right for us to preach against the issue and not give people hope to walk through that struggle.

Conclusion

This is just a brief discussion of how to do it, but my encouragement to you is to make sure that you're approachable, accessible, and that you're kind and compassionate. We're not letting down the standard. God's standard of sexuality is absolutely clear. Sex is to be expressed only between a husband and a wife within the bonds of marriage. That marriage is for life. We're clear on that. We're not letting down that standard at all. But we want to have compassion on those who are not in that situation or struggle in that situation so that they can fulfill their duties to the Lord in singleness, as they're living in celibacy, and also to their spouse, if they're married. And so that all of us, in whatever situation God has placed us in, are being faithful and honoring Christ, living out the gospel in our lives so that the Lord Jesus has the glory. He died to defeat sin, and we want to help each other do that. It's one of the main tasks of the pastor, and when we do that, we're going to pastor well.

17

What Are Permanent Disqualifications from the Ministry?

I want to discuss what could be permanently disqualifying for a pastor in ministry. In other words, what sin would permanently disqualify a pastor from ever being able to serve again?

Unrepentant Sin

First of all, I would say any unrepentant sin. We don't need to talk about categories of sin as much as we need to talk about sin being perpetuated in our lives. It is essential as a pastor of one of the Lord's churches that we stay fervent in prayer and that we stay fresh in our walk with the Lord.

If there's any sin in my life that I'm unwilling to let go of, the reality is I shouldn't be serving the Lord's church. When Paul talked about sitting at the Lord's table, he told the church at Corinth that anyone who takes this in an unworthy manner eats and drinks damnation to himself. He said many of them were sick, and some even died because of this. Now, that's when he's writing to the church members at Corinth for the way they partake of the Lord's Supper in an unworthy manner. If that's true of church members, how much more so is that true of the pastor who's administering the Lord's Supper? If he is serving the Lord's Supper in an unworthy manner because he's harboring sin in his heart and life that he knows is there, and he will not repent, that's a very serious matter.

Our consciences should be so sensitive that we do not want to hold on to sin. Our attitude should always be, "Lord, please cleanse me." If we are holding onto our sin, we have no business standing in the pulpit. We have no business administering the ordinances. A pastor who is unrepentant in his sin needs to step aside. To the degree that you are remaining willfully in sin, you should be disqualified from ministry.

When Sin Is Greater than Reputation

I know the question asks more than that, so what is permanently disqualifying? Anything that is such a breach in a pastor's life that the knowledge of that sin becomes greater than the pastor's reputation and character. So, most commonly, I get asked this about adultery. If a pastor commits adultery, can he ever serve as a pastor? This answer requires nuance. In most cases, probably not, and that's a strange answer. But frankly, I think that you can never pastor so long as your sin is notorious and so long as it becomes the thing people know about you. Only if you have walked the long, hard road of repentance so clearly, so transparently, and for so long a time can your reputation as a repentant person dominate your reputation as a sinner. I don't know how long that is, but I know it's a long time, and your repentance has to become more notorious than your sin.

So How Long?

Often, I've dealt with pastors who've fallen into sin, most notably adultery, and they immediately ask the question, "How long do you think it will be before I can preach again?" If I hear that question, I know they're nowhere close to being ready to pastor or preach again because that can't be the goal. Your goal must be to get your relationship right with the Lord. Your goal must be restoration. If you're married, to restore that relationship, to reconcile to the one you've wronged, and to forsake the sin and the weaknesses or the underlying causes of that sin. It usually doesn't happen suddenly.

When people would remark about some pastor who fell in sin and say, "Well, look how far he fell," Adrian Rodgers would always say, "You don't know how low he was living." Boy, that's true. Usually, it's not a far fall. Usually, there have been secret compromises, things happening behind the scenes in a man's life, and then when the public fall comes, it wasn't that far from all the secret things he was already doing. You need to make sure that you've dealt with all of it. It's not merely the very public disastrous crash that is the issue. It's all the stuff that led to it and was behind it. That takes a long time. So, frankly, I'm going to say that if a pastor falls into sin, his goal should not be to get back into ministry or in the pulpit. It should be simply to get right with the Lord and to do whatever it takes to demonstrate that.

Here are some things to watch out for. If a person falls into sin, even if they claim they are repentant, they may get judgmental about other people's reactions to their sin. They may say things like, "Well, look at that: he calls himself a Christian, but he's not able to forgive me for what I did." As long as you judge someone else's reaction to your sin, you're not in repentance yet. You have to own it. You have to be willing to say, "You know what? My sin is so bad that nothing that guy thinks about my sin is as bad as the truth." When you have that kind of brokenness and humility over your sin, then you're walking the road of repentance, and you have to walk it relentlessly. That's not a short time. That's a long time.

You Can't Restore Yourself

The other thing you need to know is that you can't restore yourself. You don't get to declare yourself ready or restored. There needs to be an accountability group around a preacher who falls. A group who walks with him and helps him understand the depth of his sin and what his sin has caused. Often, he can't stay in the church where the sin was committed, but he needs to plug into some church that will accept him, in essence, already under discipline, and then walk him through that repentance. But others must declare he's ready for something. But you know what? That ministry might be going to the nursing home. It might be going on trips with the senior citizens. You don't immediately get to go back up in a pulpit. It might be that someone with full knowledge of your sin might give you some opportunity. When a pastor falls into sin, it's an egregious thing because he's a leader, and his sin has effects far beyond his life or even his family. Others are hurt. Others are wounded by what he does, and that's no small thing.

It very well may be that he can never, ever again fill a pulpit. It might be that his sin is so notorious that no one can ever hear him without thinking of it. And if so, that's the cost that comes, and it's a terrible price to pay. It's one reason we should all want to stay holy because we see the terrible cost it will bring. But if, in God's providence, after some long period, after someone's repentance becomes more notorious than their sin, they are asked to fill a role, then it very well may be that they have that opportunity. I'm not going to say "never". I am going to say "rarely" because our leadership matters so much, and a lot of people can be wounded by a pastor's sin. These parameters require wisdom and I do not know exactly where they are in every case, but I do know that sin is terrible. Leadership matters so much that our goal simply must be to get right with Christ. If God, in his providence, allows us ever to have any form of ministry again, that's grace upon grace, but you can't grasp for it. You can't ask for it, and you can't do it secretly. It would have to be done with full knowledge of one's past.

A Warning

Grace is a wonderful thing, and God is gracious. It should be enough for us that our names are written in the Book of Life and that we can find a way to bring glory to Jesus, even if it's in a different kind of ministry, not in a public ministry. The goal has to be to honor him. This is such a warning to me. It reminds me of how desperately I need Christ and how much I want to live a holy life because I never want to have to ask that question. I must walk with the Lord Jesus, I lean on him constantly, I rely on the power of the Holy Spirit, I'm saturated with his Word, and I don't ever have to make someone ask the question of whether I am ready or not. God, help me by the power of the Spirit. I want to pastor well for life.

18

Should I Marry Two Non-Believers?

I like to talk about issues and answer the questions that pastors face in ministry every day, and I'm frequently asked this question in my pastoral ministry class and by other pastors: should I marry two non-believers to one another? My answer to this question might surprise you. I talk to a lot of pastors, and their initial reaction, even a strong reaction, is no — they won't marry two non-believers. If you don't have time to do it, I get it. A wedding takes a lot of time. One year, I had 26 weddings and got my fill of them. But I'm a great believer in marriage. Weddings have their place and purpose, and they serve as a marker, a testimony of the covenant of marriage.

God's Gift for All Humanity

I want to remind you of something: marriage is God's gift to humanity, not just to believers. So, I'm going to say that if you have the time and the opportunity, and if it pleases you, it's certainly not wrong for you to marry two non-believers to one another. I would say that this allows you to really speak into their lives and to have influence with them that you wouldn't have otherwise.

Now, let me be clear: I don't think you should lower your standards of premarital counseling for two non-believers. While I was in seminary, I pastored a church right beside the county courthouse. I can't tell you how many times people would knock on the door, and they had just gone to the courthouse, gotten a license, and were just looking for a preacher to tie the knot. I would not do that because I know nothing of their circumstances. I don't know if they're doing it legally. I don't know if they have the right idea of marriage or anything. But if a couple comes to me, and they're in our community, and they say, "We'd like you to marry us" — "We watch you on TV," or "We've seen you on the internet," or whatever their reason might be — and they want me to do it, assuming that I have the time, I think it's a reasonable thing for me to say, "I'm happy to do this, but here are my conditions." And I would tell them, in my case, that they must agree to eight hours of premarital counseling. Now, a lot of that is on video, but about an hour and a half to two hours of that is personal.

Counseling a Lost Couple

The way that I would approach my premarital counseling with a lost couple is to tell them they need to know that they're starting out at a great disadvantage because they can relate to one another emotionally and physically, but they aren't relating to each other spiritually. That's the most important dimension. As you go through your life, your body will change, and your status will change. A lot of things will change about you throughout a lifetime. But if you aren't spiritually bound to one another, you'll find that ten years from now, you're married to a stranger. I would take the time then to share with them the gospel and tell them why it's so important that both of them become followers of Jesus Christ. As you follow him together, you'll find that this binds you together so much more strongly than anything else possibly could. I'm really going to share the gospel with them strongly and urge them to make Jesus the Lord of their lives and of their marriage.

Now, let's say they respect my opinion but don't want to be followers of Jesus; they just want to get married. I would say that I'd still marry them, but I cannot be less than honest — several times during this counseling, they are going to hear me say, "This is going to be so much harder for you." If they no longer want me to marry them, that's okay; I'm not offended by that. I am a minister of the gospel of Jesus Christ, and when I pronounce them husband and wife, I do so in two ways. I do so because I'm an agent of the Commonwealth of Kentucky where I would do that wedding, and I do it by the authority of the Commonwealth of Kentucky because they got their license from the Commonwealth of Kentucky. But I also do it as a minister of the gospel of Jesus Christ. And that one, to me, is far more important. If they don't want me to do it because I'm so committed to sharing the gospel and being honest with them that they're going to be at a great disadvantage, that's okay.

I would share with them the necessity of following Christ. I would tell them testimonies of people who were following Jesus and the way it affected their marriage and of people who weren't, and then when they got saved, their marriage changed. I would use everything I knew to plead with them to put their faith and trust in Christ.

A Believer and a Non-Believer?

Now, I will tell you a much more difficult situation is with a believer. And I know most of you would say, "Well, I would never marry a believer and a non-believer." I will tell you there's one circumstance that I can think of where I would, and that is if a couple started attending your church, and they have four kids. They have kids, and after some time, you learn that they've been together for 15 years.

They've had these four children together, but they're not married. And let's say that the woman gets saved, trusts Christ, and comes to you and says, "I've trusted Christ, and I want to follow Christ, and my husband or my partner says that I'm free to do that. He has no objection to me doing that but wants no part of Jesus. Will you marry us?" She wants to be a follower of Jesus. That means she wants to be baptized and needs to be obedient in marrying the father of her children. In a situation like that, I think you've got two bad things colliding, which is worse. I don't think that it's a good thing to deprive those children of their father in the home. And in that case, I would say, "Okay, first of all, in every aspect other than the legal entity of marriage, they already are one flesh. I don't think it's wise to rip them apart when they have had children together." In that situation, because she wants to follow Christ and she wants to be obedient as a follower of Jesus, and she knows she needs to be married, I would marry them.

If he did object to her following Jesus, and if they didn't have kids, that would be different. But that is one circumstance I can think of where I would marry them. These are the kinds of sticky situations pastors often find themselves in. Sometimes, we're just trying to figure out what's the least bad thing to do. It's not ideal because they are already together, and he's not a believer. They already have children. Most of the time, I would say a believer shouldn't marry an unbeliever, but when they already have children together, I think it's a worse thing to rip that home apart and deprive the children of the presence of their biological father when he's willing to be in the marriage.

It Won't Get Easier

These are the kinds of things that we pastors face. And it's not getting easier. It's getting tougher. The whole issue of marriage and matrimony is more difficult to face than it's ever been before. I think it's important that we uphold the biblical standards that it's between a man and a woman and that they are covenanted together in the bonds of matrimony until God, by death, separates them. Anytime you can use premarital counseling as a means of sharing the gospel, I would encourage you to do so. I think you're free to marry two non-believers. This is the kind of thing that we all must seek the Lord about. But these are the kinds of things I like to talk about and the questions I like to answer because they're real-life situations, and I pray that the Lord will bless this to your heart so that you may pastor well.

19

How Can I Lead a Missions-Minded Church?

How can you keep your church focused on missions or become missions-minded, as we call it? How do you do that? Well, there's no shortcut.

Talk About It

You do have to talk about it a lot. First, this should not be difficult because the Bible is primarily about God's mission of redeeming his people. Furthermore, how God uses us to fulfill that mission and the Great Commission should be paramount in our minds and our preaching. This can be incorporated into your church in a number of ways. One way is to think about the way you take up mission offerings now. Giving your money is the easiest way to support missions. Other things are far more difficult, but everybody can give something to missions, and you need to ask your people to do it.

It's certainly true in our Southern Baptist churches through supporting the Cooperative Program. A certain percentage of our dollars go to the Cooperative Program, and that goes to missions, and that's great. I'm a great believer in that and believe it's a wonderful mechanism by which we regularly support missions, but people don't always feel ownership of it. That's why special missions efforts and special missions giving helps create that missions spirit and atmosphere in your church.

At Christmas in our Southern Baptist church, we take up the Lottie Moon Christmas offering for international missions. At Buck Run, we give a very large offering every year. Last year, our offering was over a hundred thousand dollars. For a church our size, that is quite significant. I challenge them every year at Christmas: "Give more to missions than you spend on any single person at Christmas time. If indeed Christmas is about celebrating the incarnation, the coming of our Lord Jesus Christ into this world, if it is representative of his birthday, then make it about him, and don't spend more on anybody in your life than you give to honor the Lord Jesus." Our people receive that challenge. I think it's a great way to challenge them because it's proportional.

People who don't have that much to spend on their kids have less to give obviously to missions as well, but it still tells them to make it about Jesus. People who have more money can give more, but they still make it about Jesus. And as a result, we have a large Christmas offering, and that has become part of the fabric of our church life. It's one way that regularly we're challenging our people to make it about the Lord and make it about missions.

Adopt Missionaries

Another thing we do is adopt missionaries. Are there missionaries that you and your church can get behind in their ministry? You can support them in helpful ways on the field. You can go visit them on the field. Our church has two IMB missionaries who are in Panama, and we regularly send teams down there.

One year, I had some budget money left over, and I went down to see them at Christmas just to spend a day with them and say, "Hey, what can I do for you? How can I pour into you?" And that missionary said that was one of the most gratifying things anyone's ever said to him.

Mission Trips

People ask about mission trips a lot, including missionaries. I hear missionaries on the field say they don't like mission trips because when churches send teams, they cause more trouble than they're worth. Well, it's your job to make sure that's not so. How do you do that? Well, if you send a team on a mission trip, you need to make sure that they are alleviating suffering problems rather than contributing to them. When we take trips, we make sure we have several meetings ahead of time, and we stress that this is not Christian tourism. This is not about getting an experience. This is not about having stories to tell. We've got specific jobs that we've been asked to do, and we're going to do those. And we tell everybody every time: "The one thing we can promise you is that this will not go as planned."

There's always stuff that happens on the mission field. People get sick. People get worms. I could tell you lots of stories. Of course, most of my experience is in the Amazon in South America, and I've had about everything you can get in the Amazon in South America, and that's what it costs to get the gospel to people. Our people need to learn that there's a cost involved in taking the gospel to people. When you take a mission trip, make sure that people understand it's not about us or our experience. It's about the mission.

Send Missionaries

Every church should be saturated with prayer that the Lord would raise up your best and your brightest from among your midst. I remember when I began to pray at Buck Run that the Lord would take our very best and our brightest. Then he took our executive pastor and his family and a man in our church who was a local high school principal. We had so many kids coming to our church because of that principal's gospel influence, and he went with our executive pastor out to Colorado to start a church. Five families went. They were our best and our brightest. God had answered my prayer. It cost us; we miss them to this day. But a church in Colorado exists now because the Lord took our best and our brightest, and now they're planting another church.

That happens because you pray for it to happen. It happens because you lay it all on the altar and say, "Lord, you take what's yours." The Old Baptist Union in England a hundred years ago used to have a symbol, an emblem, and it was an ox between an altar and a plow. It said, "Ready for either." That's the way I think our churches need to live — being ready if the Lord wants to put us in harness so that we work in the fields or if he wants to put us on the altar of service so that we go. Everything that we have belongs to the Lord Jesus. Our people are not ours. Our church is not ours. They're part of the mission. And the more you proclaim that and preach that and teach that, the more you'll see the Lord calling people out.

How did Jesus teach us to pray? He said, "Pray that the Lord of the harvest will send forth laborers." Sometimes, we make our prayer more about the Lord growing our church. That's not the purpose. We don't want to just get big and bloated. We want to send people out so that they're taking the gospel to the ends of the earth.

Don't Be Selfish

The other thing I would tell you, as a pastor, is that you really need to quit being selfish and free people up to give to things other than merely through your church. Now, that feels scary to a pastor. We get in our minds that if people start giving to other ministries, they'll give less to the church, and we'll have financial problems. My experience is exactly the opposite. When you are stingy with the Lord's people and the Lord's money, you're going to have less. When you cast your bread upon the waters, and you encourage your people to give, if there's a ministry that God lays on their heart that is doctrinally sound and teaching and preaching the gospel, trust that they won't do it at the expense of their home congregation.

It works hand in hand, arm in arm, that if they get burdened for the mission, they'll give more. Take them on a mission trip. When they see lostness, they'll want to do more. And if you are a Southern Baptist, you need to talk it up. I am such a believer in our mission programs — the Cooperative Program, the International Mission Board, and the North American Mission Board. The way we're planting churches, the way that we cooperate to train pastors and missionaries in our seminaries — I am a believer. But it's not enough for you to just put that in your budget. Your people need to own it. They need to buy into it. They need to see the investment that they're making.

Finally, tell the stories. Tell the stories of what God is doing through your people. Share testimonies. I learned a long time ago that you reproduce what you honor, and if you honor people for going, for giving, for sending, and for being faithful in the mission, then you'll reproduce more of it. The more you focus on that mission, the more mission buy-in you'll have. It's just the way it works. What did Jesus talk about? He talked about the mission, and he talked about the lost. He gave the Great Commission. What does the Book of Acts talk about? It talks about the mission of being witnesses to him in Jerusalem, Judea, Samaria, and the uttermost parts of the world. We've got to keep that strategy going in our churches and in our people. And when we do that, we'll pastor well.

PART 5

Love Well

The Pastor and His Family

20

How Can I Cultivate and Protect My Marriage?

How and why should a pastor cultivate and protect his marriage? Well, I want to note the obvious.

God's Design for Marriage

First, it's biblical. It is precisely God's design in creation. The Bible begins with a wedding, and it ends with a wedding. Jesus's first miracle is at a wedding. Marriage is a major theme in the Bible. God's design is reflected in the garden when he puts a man and a woman there and tells them to be fruitful and multiply. Marriage is, first of all, a reflection of God's glory and intentionality in the home. Nowhere should that be truer than in the pastor's home. It's also a reflection of God's design in the gospel. God could have chosen to say his love for the church is like a mother's love for her child. Instead, in Ephesians 5, he said that husbands are to love their wives as Christ loved the church, and wives are to respect their husbands and submit to them as the church does to Christ. Therefore, when we cultivate our marriages, we're reflecting God's glory in the gospel and in the consummation of the age.

In the book of Revelation, the union of Jesus and his people is portrayed as that great wedding where we will be united with him. A pastor who has a good marriage reflects God's glory in the garden and creation and in the gospel, as well as his love for the church in glory at the consummation. So, for God's glory, you need to cultivate and protect your marriage because God demands it, and he deserves it.

God's Standard for Pastors

Second, it's hard to minister to others when you have this gaping issue in your own life. I can honestly tell you that after years of serving as a pastor, outside of the authority of the Word of God itself, the single most significant source of credibility and authority that I have is my marriage. Many times throughout the decades, people have said something to me like, "I want to listen to you because I want what you and your wife have." People are looking to see if what you are preaching works. If it's not working in your home, they don't think you should be exporting it — so you need to focus on keeping your marriage vibrant and godly.

God's Plan for Holiness and Happiness

Third, cultivate your marriage for your own holiness and your own happiness. Marriage certainly is a sanctifying institution. God gave it to us as a means of holiness. Now, there's the obvious aspect of it in the physical relationship in marriage — that is, the proper expression of our sexuality in that intimate way — and that indeed does contribute toward our holiness. I also think a well-regulated physical relationship between a husband and a wife, and especially between a pastor and his wife, is a sanctifying thing. It's sanctifying in a lot of ways by the selflessness that is required in marriage. I'm learning how to give myself every day, and if I'm not willing and able to give myself to my wife at home, I'm probably not going to be that willing and able to give myself in the right way for my church.

Also, my wife is my most faithful friend and critic. I mean that in the best possible sense. I trust her opinion more than anyone. I trust her opinion about my preaching, my leadership, and my interaction with people. God put her in my life to sharpen me, to help me be more like Christ; and in the iron-sharpening process of marriage, she has helped me grow in holiness and sensitivity to people.

I still have an awful lot of rough edges, but I have fewer because Tanya York has worn them down quite a bit. I'm an introvert and could easily just sort of be a study rat, but being married to an extrovert and a people-person like Tanya has been a compelling force in my life. I need to grow and be more like her. The Lord is so good in the way he puts us together with people who complement us.

Marriage is also supposed to be a source of joy in the same way we have joy in our relationship with Christ. Churches will come and go, and it's good if you love your church. But you can get another church. That church that loves you right now could fire you next year. That's just a part of being a pastor. Your wife, however, is going to be with you through thick or thin. At least, that's the goal, so you need to cultivate your relationship with her because that needs to be primary over your relationship with the church. If you get that out of order, it will hurt you and your ministry.

So, cultivate your relationship with your wife so you both have this mutual joy and respect. I like having someone who's going through life with me just to enjoy the sunset, traveling, and meals. I want to cultivate that relationship so there's always joy in it. When I get up, in the first moments of the day, we're together. We try to make those moments special. At the end of the day, we don't dump on each other. We don't talk about all the terrible things that happened in our day or who we're upset with. We always make those pleasant moments.

We go to bed together. I'm not going to make that a hard and fast rule as if, somehow, you're ungodly if you don't do that. I used to stay up working at night for years, and I think I made a mistake. I like going to bed with my wife. I can get up as early as I want. If I want to get up at four o'clock and study, I can do that, but it's good for us to get in bed together. We have those moments together before we both drift off to sleep. We cultivate these moments of sharing and encouraging one another by saying kind things to each other — the negative stuff is off-limits. We choose when we're going to deal with those things.

God's Call to Invest

Finally, for your credibility, you need to invest in your marriage because you can't preach to other people when they look at your marriage and see that it's not working at home.

Years ago, Walmart had its initial public offering of stock, which was $16 for one share of it. Let's imagine that you bought 100 shares of

Walmart stock in 1973. You would have invested $1,600, and if you had held onto that with all its splitting and growth over the years, it would be worth close to $18 million today, give or take a million. Now, I was alive in 1973, and I'd even saved up that much as a 13-year-old. But I don't have $18 million today because I didn't invest it. You can't get a return on an investment you don't make. If you want to have a joyful marriage, you must invest in it. You are going to have to give it time and attention. You can't let your wife feel like she's somehow second place to the church.

You love the Lord Jesus first, then your wife, then your children, and then your church. Get that in the right order. You want to have balance in your life, but your wife is going to be the greatest evidence that the gospel you preach in the pulpit works in your home. So, make that investment, and you'll get the dividend.

Love Your Wife More Than Ministry

A few years ago, a friend of mine called and said he had to confess something. He said that he loved his ministry and enjoyed his church. Then he said that he loved his wife but didn't feel like he needed her. "Nothing's wrong," he said. He would get up in the morning thinking about church and preaching and wouldn't really think about his wife. He asked for advice, and I said, "You need to go to your wife, get on your knees in front of her, and beg for her forgiveness." It sort of shocked him. I told him that this was no small thing. He was thinking that just because he was not committing adultery, he was okay. If you persist in that attitude, Satan is going to bring some real destruction to your life and your home.

Trust me on this. You need to keep a flame of love and passion in your heart for your wife. I tell you the same thing that I told my friend that day. If you've allowed your marriage to get stale while you're studying sermons, teaching classes, visiting the sick, and dealing with all this stuff you deal with daily, but you're allowing the primary human relationship in your life to grow cold, you must repent. Ask God to give you the grace to be the kind of husband and leader to her that makes her glad she married a man who is now in ministry.

God will use you more publicly when you're devoted to him through your love and affection for your wife privately. Then, you will pastor well.

21

Should I Relocate My Family for a Ministry Calling?

I'm committed to pastors staying a long time at a church, if at all possible, but it's not always possible and not always the will of God. God does move people around. One of the things that you must consider, and a concern I often hear from pastors, is the impact of moving on your family.

Discerning God's Will

It's not fleshly to consider things that matter to your family when you are discerning the will of God. It's not wrong to think about things like schools and whether a new place of service can pay you a living wage. All of that comes into your calculation of whether to accept a position. They aren't the main determining factors, but frankly, God doesn't just give it to us in an engraved invitation. He usually does it in practical ways. Do we feel a fit? Is this the right time? Can we make a living? All of those things come into play. One of the most incredibly important factors in a move is its impact on your family. Pastors often face this concern with their children. It's asking a lot of your children to uproot and move and change friends and schools.

Sometimes, pastors fear that they will make their children resent the Lord or ministry and even reject the faith. I want to encourage you to truly make honoring Christ your primary goal. That needs to become the one thing you want more than anything else. It needs to be more than money, pastoring a big church, or making a name for yourself. If you just pray, "Lord, I want to glorify Jesus, and I'm willing to do anything you want me to do, but I need you to give me some clarity about what that is," I'm convinced that God will never say no to that prayer. Make that your number one prayer. Then, within that, you're looking at the practical matters. I encourage you not to make the effect on your children the primary thing. If God calls you, and if it's really for his glory for you to go, it is as much his will for your wife and your children to go.

From Julien to Detroit

Let me share some of my story with you. I grew up in Western Kentucky. My dad pastored a little church called Julien Baptist Church. Julien is in Christian County. It's nothing much more than a crossroads and a farm community. A sign used to say, "Julien, Population 18." So, that's where I was saved and baptized, and I loved it. I grew up hunting and fishing, working on farms, and enjoying my school and my friends. When I was 15, one August night, my dad asked me to come outside with him. Now, there were no streetlights at Julien, and the August sky was ablaze with the stars. You could see the Milky Way clearly, with no light pollution whatsoever. Dad and I began to talk about how beautiful it was. In the course of the conversation, he said to me, "I'm accepting the call to pastor a church in Detroit."

I was stunned. He said the Lord was leading him to go to Detroit. I said, "I can't argue with you about God's will for you, but I don't think it means I have to go there." I had an older sister who was married and lived in that community, and I said that I could live with her and her husband. I had not asked them permission to do it, but I thought I could maybe talk them into it. I was a sophomore in high school, and I didn't want to leave the friends I'd had since first grade. My dad looked at me, and he said, "Hersh if God wants me there, he wants you there just as much." I said, "I can't speak about what God wants you to do, but I don't think God cares whether or not I'm there." He said, "Well, I disagree with you, and I'm your dad, and you're going." And I knew there was no arguing with him. I knew I was going to have to go. And frankly, it was one of the hardest things. No doubt, it was the hardest thing I'd ever done to that point.

We moved to Eight Mile, and I went to the same school Eminem later went to. It was completely different from what I had ever experienced in my life, and I was determined not to like it. I was angry. I remember my dad taking me to school that first day, going into the principal's office, and the principal asked about my background and got a copy of my transcript. I remember him dismissing my dad and walking me to my first class. There were two classes left before lunch that morning, and I went to my first class. Most seats were taken. The teacher pointed out an open desk and told me to sit there. It was the same thing in the second class period that I went to. But then came lunch. There was no assigned seating for lunch. No teachers were in the cafeteria. This was the thing I most dreaded. I'm the new kid, and I talk funny. I had this Southern accent, and people looked at me funny. It was everything that you can imagine a 15-year-old felt. When I got my tray, I looked around the room; most tables were taken in the very back of the cafeteria, but there was an open table. And that's where I went. I made a beeline for it.

I faced the wall with my back to the rest of the cafeteria, where all the kids were. And I began to eat all to myself, just trying to get through lunch, when I felt a group of older school kids, like juniors and seniors, standing there beside me. One of them spoke up, and he didn't say it threatening; he just said it rather, as a matter of fact, "You're sitting at our table." And I said, "Man, I'm sorry. Look, I'm new here. Today's my first day. And if you would be so kind as to let me sit here, I won't bother you. Tomorrow I won't be here, but please don't ask me to move because I don't know where else to sit. Can I just sit here for today?" He looked at me and said, "You're from the south, aren't you?" He had recognized my accent. I said, "Yeah, I am." He asked what state, and I answered Kentucky. He said, "What part of Kentucky?" I said, "Western Kentucky." And then asked, "Near Hop Town?"

Now, Hop Town is the insider language for the county seat of Christian County. I grew up near Hopkinsville, and people from there call it Hop Town. This startled me. And I said, "Yes, near Hop Town. I lived out in the country but in Christian County." He said, "Do you know where Newstead is?" This was unbelievable. I told you I lived in Julien. Julien was just a little crossroads, and the very next crossroads was Newstead, again, population 18 or something like that. It's no bigger than Julien, but this guy knew it. And I said, "Yeah, I know Newstead." And he said, "Do you know Wink Roberts?"

My mouth dropped open. I said, "My dad pastored a little baptist church there at a place called Julien, and Wink Roberts was one of the three deacons in my dad's church. I've known Wink Roberts my whole life." This kid said, "That's my uncle Wink. You can sit here. You're good, man." Suddenly, I was in with the cool kids. These were the cool kids. These were the gifted kids. They were musically inclined, they were upperclassmen, and they were athletes. They were the popular kids in school. And here I was, a kid from Kentucky, on my first day sitting at the table with them, and they became my peer group. I had a connection with them. I'll never forget going home that day. My mom and dad were nervous, and they were dreading the worst, afraid I would come home miserable.

I walked in the door, and my dad asked, "Well, how was your first day?" And I told him that he wouldn't believe it but that I had met Wink Robert's nephew. I said that I felt right at home, and the kids were so nice to me. I had a great first day and will tell you that my experience there at Lincoln High School in Warren, Michigan, was great. I got a full tuition scholarship to Michigan State University, and God did incredible things in my life. He made my world much bigger than it otherwise would've been. It really was the hardest thing I could have done at that point in my life, but it was also the best thing. God used that to make me able to talk to just about anybody. Are you from the South? Me too. Are you from the north? Me too. Are you from the country? So am I. Are you from an urban culture? So am I. I can't tell you the doors that have opened for me.

And what God taught me on that day in 1975 as a 15-year-old sophomore is that he goes before me, and I can trust him. When he leads me somewhere, I don't go alone. It not only was an encouragement to me, but it reminded me that God leads us as families.

Conclusion

If he puts you somewhere, your job is to shepherd your kids and to get them to see that we're pursuing Christ. This isn't about changing schools. This isn't about our comfort. It's about glorifying him. Your family is part of the ministry to which God has called us. If God does call you, he's calling your family too. He will teach you those lessons, and he will guide you. If your goal is to bring glory to Jesus, pray that he'll never say no to that. And then you can pastor well.

22

Should I Observe the Billy Graham Rule?

Should a pastor observe the Billy Graham rule? In other words, should a pastor ever allow himself to be alone with a woman? Well, I'm going to make it bigger than that question. I want to start by talking about a pastor's disposition toward women in general because, frankly, it's about a lot more than simply being in a room with a woman. It's about a pastor's demeanor and way of dealing with the women that he shepherds.

Find the Line, Don't Get Close

I know there are situations where pastors must counsel women. I'm never going to say that a shepherd should not do that, but I'm going to say that underneath that single event, there needs to be such a transparency of life and a purity of soul that a pastor really shows himself trustworthy. While it can be hard to define specifically, women can discern when a man is putting out inappropriate signals. Sometimes, men do this to see what kind of reaction they get and say things that are just on the edge. These things may not be inappropriate in and of themselves, and they wouldn't sound that bad if you looked at those words on a page. But when a man says things like, "You sure look good today," you've crossed the line.

My contention after more than four decades of ministry is that you can just tell when people are sort of dancing close to the line. Pastors should be nowhere near that line. One of the key strategies in my life has always been to absolutely focus on my wife. I want to love her. I want everybody to know I love her. I sort of have a Jesus and Tanya rule that if I'm around somebody for the first time, within the first fifteen minutes of knowing them, I'm going to talk about Jesus and Tanya.

And I've tried to do this for a lot of reasons. One, that's who I love. I love Jesus, and I love Tanya, and the ones that you love are going to come up in your conversation. But also, it just puts women at ease that I'm devoted to my wife, and as a pastor, I would never, ever want to make any woman uncomfortable. I would never want to project in any way that I feel toward any woman anything other than that I am a brother in Christ, a father in the Lord, a fellow Christian, and a follower of Jesus, and I don't want to do anything that messes that up. Satan is a roaring lion. He's seeking whom he may devour. He wants to devour a pastor and his ministry. And this is one of the areas where preachers need to be on guard. There needs to be such a commitment to purity, a commitment that we're never ever looking to get anywhere near that line. In essence, there should be a zone of security that we project that we're not in any way going to be inappropriate in general.

I also do my best to avoid situations that would allow anybody to think that something could occur. So yes, a woman can talk to me privately in my office, but there's glass on my door. And at Buck Run, we put all of our offices in a single suite. Our doors face one another. Everybody sees who comes in and who leaves. And I would not meet alone with a woman outside of my office. Yes, I'm going to allow women to have access to their pastor appropriately. In that professional setting, we're in my office with other people around. I would not go to the church alone and meet with a woman outside of those office hours.

If I need to meet with a woman outside of office hours, I take someone with me who can be within vision of us, even if the conversation needs to be private. Or, in the best-case scenario, I'm going to take Tanya with me. She's most often involved in any kind of counseling situations that I would have. So, I'm always looking for ways just to make sure that we're not allowing any kind of an emotional bond to build because of spending a lot of time with a woman, but I'm also not making her feel like there's anything wrong on my end. I'm looking out for her benefit and for her reputation. At the same time, I'm giving her access to her shepherd. And I think we need to do both of those things. It's not as simple as saying,

"Oh, I won't meet with a woman." Well, you're her shepherd, and she sometimes needs the counsel of her shepherd.

You're Her Shepherd

Find an appropriate place and way to do it that is not in any way demeaning to her, and that doesn't make her feel like she's untrustworthy. People understand and appreciate your desire to be completely above the board while being accessible when you are just striving for godliness in your own life. Jesus gave women access to his ministry.

This is one of the dominant things in the Gospel of Luke. When I preached through Luke, I saw so well how there were women who traveled with Jesus and the disciples. They had access to Jesus, but never in any inappropriate way. They supported Jesus and the disciples and their ministries, and Jesus loved them. He loved them appropriately. That's what I want to do. I want to let them have access to their shepherd, but I want to do it in appropriate ways that won't cast any kind of suspicion on anyone. When you do that, people appreciate it. They see your desire for holiness and the tenderness with which you do it. You're not trying to make anybody feel uncomfortable; you're just trying to be godly. And when you do that, you pastor well.

23

What are the Expectations of a Pastor's Wife?

This is one of those topics that is particularly sensitive. What are reasonable expectations of a pastor's wife? Now, that is a tough one because, first of all, we often think that a church calls a man to be a pastor, and they don't have any right to have expectations of the pastor's wife. I'm not going to deny that many churches go way overboard in what they expect of the pastor's wife and the demands they make on her. That can happen. They can go to the point of being beyond anything reasonable. But I'm also going to say that the Bible gives a church the right to have expectations of a pastor's family.

We're told in 1 Timothy 3 that a pastor has to manage his household well and that he has to have obedient children. If you're not a good steward at home, you can't be a good steward of the Lord's church and the Lord's people. So, a pastor's wife certainly is important to his ministry, but you have to account for the fact that not all pastors' wives are alike. They have different personalities, different gifts, and different skills, and you can't expect all of them to be alike.

Reasonable Expectations vs. Unreasonable Expectations

So, what are reasonable expectations of a pastor's wife? First, you are right to have the same expectations of a pastor's wife that you have of every other church member, such as expectations of attendance, serving, and giving. I don't think a pastor's wife should be any different than any other member. If you're asking members to show up and serve, give, attend, learn, and grow, that's right for the pastor's wife to do as well. At the bare minimum, I think a pastor's wife should be serving like a faithful member of that church.

I remember when Tanya and I got married, Tanya couldn't play the piano at all. She has quite a lovely voice, but it's not a solo voice. She felt bad. She couldn't play the piano and sing solos. That was sort of the expectation. Pastor's wives could play the piano and sing solos. Well, what Tanya could do is so much better than playing the piano and singing solos, but I remember her feeling that she didn't measure up. It took her a few years to grow into knowing that she didn't have to measure up.

The Need for Discretion

Be who you are. Use the gifts that God has given you. You know what I think a pastor's wife needs as much as anything? More than any skill or expectation, she needs discretion. Discretion means that she's going to have access to information and knowledge of situations that not everyone has. And she's going to have to learn not only to keep it to herself and not tell it to others but also how not to be emotionally adversely affected. There have been times in my ministry when people did hurtful things to me and said cruel things. I needed Tanya not to act out against those people out of woundedness on my behalf. I needed her to just love them and leave any kind of correction to me. It would've been harmful for her to get involved and correct people for behavior because she does not have that authority.

I am the shepherd. I have the authority to reprove, rebuke, and exhort with all patience and long-suffering — that's on me. Sometimes, she knew about things, and sometimes, she heard things, but she needed to pray for me, show discretion, and not react to the situation. A pastor's wife needs to show grace because she's often going to be tempted to feel vengeful. She's going to see people act spitefully. She's going to see people reverse themselves, and people who acted like friends then act like enemies. She needs to model grace because any other course of action will only make it harder for her husband. I need that. I don't need my wife to play the piano; I don't need her to sing; but I need her to show discretion and grace. I think it's right to expect a pastor's wife to show the fruit of the spirit, and it is so important that we understand that it's not optional equipment for any believer, certainly not for a pastor or for his wife.

We must show love, joy, and peace. We have to have that as a way of life because you can either make the situation worse by compounding it with your own sinfulness, or you can show the fruit of the spirit and calm the situation. Just don't make it worse. Let the Lord deal with those who have done wrong. Make sure that you're always walking in the spirit.

Following an Imperfect Leader

I think it's important that a pastor's wife follow her husband's leadership and realize that he's fallen and broken. He's not perfect. He's a sinner, and yet he's a sinner whom God has called and God has chosen. Now, that doesn't mean a wife shouldn't have honest conversations with her husband about his need to repent or to change. That's part of being married, especially in a Christian marriage. It means that she follows him, knowing that he's imperfect but that he's God's servant, and she wants to do everything she can to help him in that task.

Don't Let People Come Between You

I also want to warn you that people will use the pastor's wife as an information channel in both directions. Sometimes, people will be afraid to say something to the pastor, but they'll say it to his wife, or they won't ask the pastor for information, but they'll try and get it from his wife and try to influence the influencer. They'll try to get a pastor's wife to see something a certain way so that she might speak into the pastor's decision in their favor. Be aware of that. Don't let people become a wedge between the pastor and his wife. Make sure that you understand people are just going to do what people do, but you must be resolved that it's not going to come between you. It's not necessarily bad that people use the pastor's wife as an information channel, but it can be disastrous. Sometimes, you both have to be agonizingly honest about whether or not it's working and ask if you are allowing that to come between you.

She's the Pastor's Wife First

The most important thing is that the pastor's wife be the pastor's wife, be his partner in every way. She's not the co-pastor. She's his ministry partner. She's his wife. She is one flesh with him, which means that she seeks to honor, encourage, be honest with, follow, and speak honestly into his life when he needs to be corrected. I thank God for Tanya's honesty with me, and she is my most faithful critic in every way. She's also my greatest encourager. I need both things. I need to be open to her, and I need to be receptive to what she has to say. But you know what? I can get another church. I can't get another wife. And that relationship, my relationship with her, has to be more primary in my life than my relationship with my church.

I've learned that regardless of what happens out there, if I can come home and things are good between us — there's joy in our spirit, lightness in our step, and a mutual love of the Lord Jesus — then it doesn't matter what else happens out there. I can handle it because I'm coming home to her, and she's my friend. She's my faithful encourager. She's my lover. She's my ministry partner. She's my wife. When you have a great pastor's wife, it's so much easier to pastor well.

24

How Can I Guard Against Pornography?

One of the most insidious problems that we face is pornography. How can a pastor protect himself against Satan's attacks through the means of pornography? This problem is ubiquitous. I don't think anything in our culture has had a greater negative impact than pornography.

The Porn Crisis

When I was a boy, pornography was pretty much limited to magazines, and you actually had to go to a place to procure it. There were certain places that sold pornography or made it available, and people had to actively seek it and go someplace. How different that is from today. Wherever you are, if you have any kind of internet access, pornography of any kind is available to you 24 hours a day, 7 days a week. I have seen the horrific effects that this has had on the churches and our culture. I am convinced that pornography is one reason why our culture has embraced the whole LGBTQ+ movement, and I am convinced that much of the sexual confusion in our culture today is because of pornography. I've worked with missionaries, seminary students, and pastors in counseling. I no longer ask the question, "Have you ever had a problem with pornography?" I ask, "When was the last time?"

This is not a problem that is specific to Southern Seminary or seminaries in general. Every seminary, every church, and every part of our culture is touched by it. In the premarital counseling that I do, in almost every situation, one or both members of the couple will tell me that they've been terribly influenced by pornography. It has influenced our views of sexuality, of what sex itself looks like, of what the relationship between a man and a woman looks like — or worse yet, between men and men, women and women — and all of this largely because it has become so available and accessible. I don't think I need to make the case, but let me go just a little further and tell you that if you study this at all, you'll see that pornography has a terrible effect on human beings. There's a Ted Talk called "The Great Porn Experiment" by Gary Wilson, and in it, he talks about the physical response of the human brain to pornography. While Wilson does not address the issue of pornography as a Christian, everything he says is consistent with a Christian worldview and demonstrates the dangers pornography presents.

Why would a 17-year-old boy who does not know Christ not look at it if it's accessible? His curiosity is natural. Why would he not? Jesus is really the only reason why a young man or woman would not look at pornography because they understand the larger moral picture and how damaging it is. This is why the gospel matters so much. But often, when young men or women are being called into ministry or committing to the Lord, they've already been massively influenced by pornography.

Do Whatever It Takes

Pornography is ubiquitous, so how can we stop it? "How can a young man cleanse his way?" That's the question the psalmist asks, and it's the one we want to answer. What are the safeguards that you need to put into your life so that you will not fall prey to this? Well, let me just say this. You need to right now make the commitment that, whatever it takes for you to remain pure and free from this tool of Satan, you need to commit. Do whatever it takes.

In the Sermon on the Mount, Jesus talked about getting so radical as to pluck out your eye and cut off your hand. Now, people say Jesus didn't mean that literally. No, he meant it more than literally. Obviously, he did mean to get radical about holiness. It's true — plucking out your eye isn't going to solve the problem because a blind man can still lust, and cutting off your hand doesn't solve the problem because a man with no hands can still covet and even steal. You're going to have to go deeper than just your eye or your hand. You're going to have to go all the way to the heart.

You need to begin with a prayer for purity. You need to ask the Lord to cleanse your heart. How does he do that? He does it by the Word of God. You can't be in the Word and routinely in pornography at the same time. You need to be saturated with the Word of God, and if Satan begins to tempt you, turn to the Word.

Put some safeguards in place that will make you accountable. If you need to sign up for a subscription service that puts a filter on your computer, and you need an accountability partner who can see everything you're looking at, then do that. If you need to use your computer only in public spaces, then do that. If you need to make sure you don't put your computer in the back of the basement in the corner where your monitor is facing the wall and away from everybody else so you have plenty of time to blank your screen, do that. Make yourself as transparent and as accountable as you possibly can so that anybody can see what you're looking at.

The problem that I have is not so much looking at vile things as vain things. Sometimes, I shudder to think how much I'm looking at stuff about University of Kentucky basketball, for instance. It's silly stuff that is maybe a time waster, but frankly, I can't be ashamed of that so much that I don't want anybody having access to my computer. So, I want my wife to have total access to my computer. I want her to have every password to my accounts. I don't have secrets from her. She's free to look. She's free to look at my computer. She's free to ask me tough questions. She has my text messages, and anything she wants she can have. Just the accountability of knowing someone else is looking at what I'm looking at helps me with purity.

I don't want to do anything that's going to demolish my ministry. I mean, this is all I do. This is what I've trained my life for. Why would I give it away for something that is not even satisfying? All it does is create a deeper soul-wrenching hunger that cannot be satisfied. You need to make sure you have a radical commitment to holiness and will do whatever you need. Have total accountability, but frankly, it has to come out of a love for the Lord Jesus Christ.

Love Jesus More

I've had this conversation several times with young men who were addicted to pornography. I've said to them, "If I tell you that I'll give you $10,000 if you just don't look at pornography tonight, could you do it? Could you not look at pornography for this evening if I promised you $10,000?" Inevitably, they always go, "Well, yeah, for $10,000, I could do it." "Okay? Then, what we've just learned is that you do have control. It's not a matter of you having control. It's a matter of what you want more, and when you tell me you could forego looking at pornography for $10,000, you just told me you want $10,000 more than you want to look at pornography." You've got to want to honor Jesus more than you want to look at pornography. You've got to want him. You've got to want his delight.

When you get the radical commitment to honor and serve the Lord Jesus Christ, then you're going to do whatever it takes to get the thing you want more, so you're going to make yourself accountable, and you're going to let your computer habits be public, and you're going to have accountability partners. You're not going to be alone with your computer, with your phone, or whatever it might be. If you need to get a flip phone instead of a smartphone because you're looking at pornography on your smartphone, then you do it.

Do whatever you must do to be holy and godly. Is it worth building into your life that kind of deception and ungodliness? You may be hiding it from others, but it's there. And then to stand in the pulpit and look like you're godly? Is it worth it? What matters more to you, to look godly or to be godly? I want to be who Jesus wants me to be. I want my life to bring glory to him in the most secret places. At the most secret, I still want to bring honor and glory to God. Do what you need to do to be pure and holy.

I'm encouraging you to make it a matter of prayer, saturate yourself with the Word of God, and be accountable. Read Heath Lambert's book, *Finally Free*. I think that would be a great help and blessing to you. But most of all, you've got to love Jesus more. Plead with him to help you love him more, and you'll pastor well.

PART 6

Finish Well

The Pastor and His Legacy

25

How Can I Prevent Burnout in Ministry?

How can a pastor find spiritual refreshment? Burnout and dryness in ministry are an occupational hazard. We want to know how we can continue to pour into others without emptying ourselves. How can we stay fresh in our walk with Christ even as we are facing so many challenges and difficulties in ministry?

Balance

There is nothing more refreshing in your life than balance. I know that word balance is loaded because we all strive for it, and we don't know how to do it. I've learned this: whatever God calls me to do, it is not inherently in conflict with anything else he's given me to do. You need to admit that to yourself. If he's called you to be a pastor, and he's called you to be a husband and a father, those things are not inherently in conflict. It doesn't mean there won't be tension sometimes in trying to find time to do those things, but they're not inherently in conflict. If he's called you to be a pastor and a husband and a father, those things are going to work in tandem for you to accomplish the will of God. So, you want to strive for balance.

The Lord Jesus showed perfect balance in his life. He was never in a hurry. He was always on time, never late. Now, that wasn't what it looked like to other people. Other people accused him of being late. When Peter accused him, saying there were still sick people in town, Jesus said they were going on to the next town. That seemed strange to Peter. In John

11, Mary and Martha both said, "Lord, if you'd been here, our brother would not have died." They made judgments about him that were not true, but Jesus was not phased. He knew that he was living on a divine timetable. This is what pastors have to do. We have to understand that not everybody's going to get it. People are going to accuse you of not doing the thing you ought to do or doing things you ought not to do. I will tell you that in over four decades of ministry, the biggest complaints about me have not been about things I did but things I didn't do. And people will think you should do more than you're doing or think you should do things that you have not done. You're going to have to learn to live with that.

It's a sad truth but a necessary one: to be in the ministry means you have to learn how to live with people's disappointment. They're going to be disappointed in you. They're not going to get it. If it was true in the life of Jesus, it will also be true in your life. There are going to be people who say, "If you would have been here…, but you were gone." They're never going to understand. You just have to do the best you can in humility and grace to maintain the balance God's given you.

Discipline

One way you do that is by maintaining spiritual disciplines. And this is where I certainly want to commend the book written by my colleague Don Whitney on spiritual disciplines. You need to read it and practice it. Stay in the disciplines of life — reading the Bible, journaling, praying, and sharing the gospel. The more that you are actively making this your life, the more naturally this becomes the way you live.

Physical health, exercise, and getting enough sleep are important. My dad used to say, "Come apart and rest, or you'll just come apart." It's true. You see Jesus getting time alone with the Father. He had to have that personal time with the Lord and personal time with his disciples, then time with the crowds and time with individuals. Maintain a schedule where you take care of your health and get enough rest. I would urge those of you who are married to go to bed with your wives. I don't mean that in any euphemistic way. I mean, literally, don't stay up late by yourself, especially these days. There's so much temptation on the internet and television. I think it's a good discipline for you to go to bed with your wife.

You can get up as early as you want. My wife never complains that I get up early in the morning, but we like to go to bed together. That's sort of our time. We talk. We can read; we can watch TV; we can do whatever we want before we go to sleep, but it's our way of ending the day together — focused on each other. My time alone with the Lord in the morning is mine, and I get up way before she does, but that helps me maintain that balance. If you are staying up late at night and not getting enough rest, tiredness makes you not as sharp in what you do. Secondly, I think it often leads to sin of other kinds. So, maintain a good schedule, get a basic amount of exercise, and eat well. Your physical health contributes to your spiritual health.

Stewardship

Financial stewardship is also important. Take care of what God has entrusted to you. A lot of times, stress comes into our lives because we are not good stewards. We don't take care of the finances God has provided for us. So, you want to learn to guard your money, be generous, and give to the Lord's work and the Lord's causes. If you're reckless with your money, it adds stress in other areas. Again, the more unnecessary stress we allow into our lives, the more it's a breeding ground for sin. I've just seen so many times that people act out. And when people are hurt and wounded, they tend to look for comfort in things that really can't provide comfort. But Satan uses them as tools.

Refreshment

You need to learn to live a transparent life and live in such a way that your boundaries are clear to others. That helps you maintain spiritual refreshment. And then I would tell you, you need recreation and hobbies that you do alone, with others, and with your wife if you're married. I think it's good for you to always have something to look forward to, even if it's way out there. When Tanya and I were first married, we were broke. We were broke for the first 20 years we were married, and we figured out ways to do cheap or free things. We put them on the calendar, which built a rhythm in our marriage that helped us handle the difficult times and seasons because we were looking forward to getting away.

Love

It's a joy to have someone with whom I can get away and who helps me in my walk with the Lord. But I would tell you that the greatest tool I think to have spiritual refreshment is to love the Word of God and love God's people. The more I love Jesus, the more I love his Word, and the more I love his people. And the more time I spend in his Word and with his people, the more I love him. You can either get in a vicious cycle where the negative things in your life feed each other and worsen the situation, or you can get in a cycle of blessing where these joys in your life feed and sustain one another. Loving Christ means loving his Word, and spending time in his Word. You're hearing from him, and then you will want to share with his people, and it changes the way you live at home, the kind of father and husband you are, and the kind of Christian you are.

Conclusion

The way you treat people is going to be shaped by whether you're spiritually refreshed. It can undercut everything we do if we get up there and preach a great sermon, but we're spiritually empty. Years ago, I spoke for Dr. Steve Lawson in Mobile, Alabama, at a deacon banquet. Dr. Lawson and his deacons gave me a gift. They gave me a beautiful S.T. Dupont fountain pen. Man, I love that pen. I still have it. It was the first fountain pen I ever owned. It was black Chinese lacquer with a gold nib. And I was taught that gold nib adapts to the angle of your writing, so don't let anybody else use that. I mean, it is a sanctified pen. It is set apart for my use, and I was proud of that pen.

I would use that pen on Sundays. I remember one Sunday I was preaching in Louisville when, just a few moments before I got up to preach, I had one of those last-minute thoughts I needed to write down. I reached into my pocket, and I pulled out that black lacquer S.T. Dupont. I began to write on my notes, but nothing happened. I shook it. I tried again, but nothing happened. A little boy was sitting on the pew behind me, and I turned around and asked if he had a pen. He reached into his pocket and pulled out a little plastic pen with teeth marks all over it. He had just chewed on this thing, and he handed it to me, and I wrote down my thoughts with his chewed-up plastic pen then gave it back to him. And something occurred to me. That plastic chewed-up pen was better than my S.T. Dupont pen with a gold nib. If it's empty inside and there's no ink in it, it does me no good. Look, it doesn't matter how educated you are. It doesn't matter how eloquent you are. If you're empty inside, you're doing no good for the Kingdom. You need to stay full of the Spirit, immersed in the Word of God, in love with Jesus, and walking in the disciplines of life. And when you do that, to pastor well is a joy.

26

Five Ministry Challenges I Didn't Anticipate

Life and ministry have changed rapidly and radically over the past forty years. Reared in a pastor's home, I was not, on the one hand, totally unprepared for the complexities and complications that awaited me when I accepted my first full-time ministry assignment at only twenty years old. On the other hand, no one was prepared for the sweeping changes that the next four decades would produce. Five things, in particular, caught me completely unprepared and added challenges to life and ministry that I never saw coming but nonetheless to which I had to respond.

Security and Abuse Issues

When I was a boy, I spent a lot of time alone with older men who were members of churches my father served as pastor. They taught me to work hard, hunt stealthily, fish patiently, accurately identify plants and trees in the woods, and drive almost anything. None of them ever acted inappropriately or abused me in any way. They were kind, godly men who helped me walk toward manhood. Each of them proved worthy of the trust my parents placed in them. That idyllic childhood hardly prepared me for the hidden crimes and abuses perpetrated in many churches that would later be widely exposed and reckoned with.

Consequently, ministry today means thinking about physical safety issues and the price paid when that does not happen. Not only are churches now endeavoring to help those hurt in the past, but they also must do everything possible to prevent any crimes or even potential for such deeds in the future.

I did not foresee a need to run background checks on all church employees, leaders, and volunteer workers, but we do. Nor did I realize how much the physical security of church members and employees would factor into the design and expense of a new building, but it did. For the first half of my ministry, I never thought of lockdowns, active shooters, armed and uniformed officers in the church building, security cameras, or a policy that no adult may ever be alone with a child, but I certainly have in the last two decades. Like many others, I needed education and training to know how to protect the people whom I lead. That often meant hearing hard truths about consequences when churches and shepherds are not vigilant, stories so grievous that they made me resolve to do everything I could so it did not happen on my watch.

The Collapse of Coherence on Sexuality and Gender

I remember when the public relations agenda of the gay lobby could be summed up in the word "tolerance." They claimed that all they wanted was to be allowed to live their lives as they saw fit. No one asks for "tolerance" anymore. The demand now has moved beyond acquiescence or acceptance to full agreement and celebration.

Not only did the vocabulary of the demand change but so did the coalition of those demanding it. The "gay lobby" became LGBTQIA+, and the + means so many things that it's impossible to keep up: two-spirit, non-binary, pansexual, demisexual, aromantic, gender fluid, and asexual! Who saw that coming? Not I. But the most troubling thing is that neither did I anticipate that people who have claimed to be Bible-believing Christians for years would abandon clear biblical precepts to accept the views perpetrated on them by the contemporary culture. I did not foresee Christian colleges and universities abandoning the clear moral standards of their past and raising a white flag of surrender followed by a rainbow flag of assimilation. I could not have believed that parents would be led by their indoctrinated children on this issue rather than the other way around. I correctly assumed the world would gradually accept homosexuality, but I never imagined a wholesale denial of gender reality.

Some people have always argued that they should be allowed to dress and to live however they wanted, but I could not have known that much of the world would vociferously argue that genes and genitalia do not determine sex, that men can have babies, that gender can be fluid, that people have the right to force others to use certain pronouns, or that biological men can compete in women's sports. I never foresaw that a female nominee for the Supreme Court of the United States would be unable or unwilling — under oath — to define what a woman is.

In the entire history of the world, no previous culture has been confused on this issue. Whether pagan or Christian, rural or urban, ancient or modern, everyone knows how to finish the sentence uttered at the birth of a healthy baby: "It's a . . . ." I did not envisage that our culture would have the hubris to look back in smug judgment on all others and simply say, "We know better."

Screens Are Disciplers

My parents' generation complained frequently about their kids' being glued to the television. They had no idea that screens would morph and proliferate into every room, every space, and every waking moment in the lives of their grandchildren and great-grandchildren. No one foresaw that those ubiquitous screens could simultaneously bring information and inanity, delight and danger, gospel preaching and graphic pornography. No one knew that the self-image and mental health of teens would be shaped — and threatened — by the things they saw on those screens.

Opinions on everything from sex and sexuality to Christian nationalism to fashion to theology to politics and public discourse are formed largely from online exposure. Out of the same screen come praise and cursing. I don't think I am doing the biblical writer James a disservice by applying his statement on the tongue to our screens: "My brothers, these things ought not to be so" (James 3:10).

Screens on computers, iPads, cell phones, and TVs are relentlessly streaming values, opinions, worldviews, and images into the minds of believers and unbelievers alike at an informational rate many times over anything in the past. Parents are giving their children easy access to the internet and, consequently, giving everything on the internet easy access to their children. And parents are being manipulated and molded by those same forces as much as their children.

Christian ministries and churches have tried to use those screens for gospel purposes and have succeeded in many ways. Still, biblical truth proclaimed on the internet is — to paraphrase the great R. G. Lee — "like a fragrant gardenia in a garbage dump." I had no idea how much of my time in ministry would be spent dealing with people discipled destructively by a screen.

A Global Pandemic

I had read books or watched movies about what a global pandemic might look like, but I had never thought about what it might mean to lead a church through one. I did not see it coming, and when I did, I did not think it would last long. When it lasted long, I still held out the hope, even the belief, that an endpoint would come at which everything reverted to what it was before I ever heard of COVID-19. I know now that will never happen. The world has changed in ways we can neither undo nor move past. I thought the biggest problems of a pandemic would be health issues, but for me, at least, the leadership challenges were far more challenging than the three times I contracted COVID. How could I lead a church when we couldn't gather? How could we maintain unity in a world so fractured? How could the voice of a shepherd be heard above the din of everything else the sheep were seeing and listening to online? I had always trusted my ability to look my members in the eye and speak candidly and honestly so that they gave me their trust. I never thought about how I would lead when I couldn't even be with them for a while or have them all together, even when we came back in multiple services. I also didn't know that the members of my church would have such different opinions about the social and medical issues the pandemic brought.

Though the pandemic ended, many effects remain. Some church members simply disappeared, and we don't know where they went or what happened to them. Some never came back and said they were no longer following Christ. Habits and expectations changed. I am grateful our church made it through the pandemic without major divisions or disruptions, but it was hard and made me develop a different set of skills than those I relied on before.

The Vitriol Among Christians

I can name numerous evangelical leaders who shared platforms and enjoyed close fellowship ten years ago but hardly speak to each other now. Historically, theology has been the basis of Christian fellowships and denominations, but in recent years, theological distinctives have given way to myriad other issues that previously were secondary or non-existent.

Christians don't merely disagree about theology or the best way to be Christian in a multicultural, pluralist society. They argue about politics, vaccines, the war in Ukraine, race, and a host of other matters that, though important, were once left out of church spaces.

Those disagreements lead to suspicions of a departure from faithfulness and fidelity. Those suspicions, in turn, embolden public accusations and personal animus, including labels intended to demean and dismiss someone over a single issue. Fellowship has fractured over non-theological issues like never before in my lifetime. And if that is true on the broad spectrum of evangelicalism, it is equally true in local churches.

Social media provides a public platform for everyone, and Christian charity is often the first casualty when an indignant believer feels justified in publicly correcting or calling out someone. The more outrageously the outrage is expressed, the more hits or views it generates. I confess that I did not anticipate this degree of animosity among believers, particularly between well-known leaders.

While I must admit a lack of foresight and being completely shocked by these major developments over the course of my ministry, one thing I saw very clearly, and which has only been confirmed across decades of experience, is this: the gospel of Jesus Christ is true. I have frequently been disappointed by people, even more so in myself, but Jesus has never let me down. Through all the sadness, confusion, disappointment, misinformation, and animosity around me, I still know that the gospel is the deepest need for the greatest problem in the world. I am more determined than ever to believe it, preach it, tell it, trust it, and live it than ever before — no matter what comes next.

THE
SOUTHERN BAPTIST
THEOLOGICAL SEMINARY

SBTS.EDU